A Sane Approach to Database Design

A Sane Approach to Database Design

By Mark Johansen

Lulu * Morrisville, North Carolina

A Sane Approach to Database Design
© 2008 by Mark Johansen.

D. B. Monkey cartoons by Ryan Adamson.

Cover photo © 2007 by iStockphoto.com / Elena Vdovina. Used under license.

This publication includes images from Corel Gallery™ Magic 65,000 which are protected by the copyright laws of the U.S., Canada, and elsewhere. Used under license.

Oracle, MySQL, Postgres, Access, mySQL, DBase, FoxPro, Word, ERWin, Visio, and CorelDraw are trademarks of their respective owners.

Questions or comments about this book may be directed to the author at sanedb@electrictactics.com.

ISBN: 978-1-4357-3338-1

Table of Contents

Detail Contents

1. INTRODUCTION

*For, usually and fitly, the presence of an introduction is held
to imply that there is something of consequence and
importance to be introduced.*

-- Arthur Machen

This book is about how to design a database.

There is a difference between knowing which end of a hammer to
hold and being a skilled carpenter. There is a difference between
knowing what the gas pedal and the steering wheel are for and being a
champion race car driver. There is a difference between knowing SQL
and being a skilled database designer.

Knowing how to use the tools is certainly a requirement to being
skilled in an art, but it is not sufficient. It is just the first step.

Many aspiring database designers get confused on this point. They
think that "knowing SQL" and "knowing how to design a database"

are the same thing. The fact that someone managed to hack something together that sort of mostly worked does not mean that he or she knows how to do it right. Just like the fact that he managed to drive from his home to his office without being arrested or demolishing the car in an accident does not mean that he is qualified to be a race car driver. I do not mean this to belittle the efforts of someone struggling to get the job done with little or no study or training. Quite the contrary. If he managed to hack away and get a database to work just on what he could figure out on his own, congratulations to him! Maybe if he kept plugging away at it, eventually he would figure out all the techniques and tricks of the trade that have been accumulated by people who have been doing it for years. But let's face it: Unless he is the greatest computer genius in history, chances are he is not going to figure out on his own what has taken hundreds of people the past twenty or thirty years to figure out. Why not benefit from the experience of others?

The fact that you are reading this book indicates that you are interested in learning and improving your skills. That's an excellent step to take. Whether you are a beginner just trying to learn the basics, or if you've been doing it for years and are looking for ideas on how to do it better, I believe this book can help you.

I use SQL for examples and illustrations because SQL is very popular, so SQL examples are most likely to be relevant. But 90% of the contents of this book apply whether you are using SQL or some other language.

This book is not about questions like, "What is the syntax of the SQL create index statement?", but "How do I know what data to put in the database?" and "How should I organize the database?" The details of language structure and syntax are certainly important, and if that's what you're looking for right now, this is not the book for you.

But I believe we should answer the big questions first. There's little point in agonizing over which shoes to wear to church until you have decided whether or not you believe in God. The second most important question to answer in life is what database design methodology you will use. In this book I hope to help you find answers to that question.

2. STYLE CONVENTIONS

Never offend people with style when you can offend them with substance.

-- Sam Brown

2.1. Introduction

There are a few style conventions I use in this book to avoid confusion.

2.2. Code Examples

Examples of computer code and commands are given in a typewriter font. Literal text, that is, text that you would type in exactly as shown, is printed upright. Variable text, which you will replace with something specific to your situation, is given in italics.

For example:

```
select column from table
```

"select" and "from" are literal text that must appear exactly as shown; "column" and "table" would be replaced with your own text.

When there is a group that repeats, I put ellipses: "...".

Example:

```
select column, … from table
```

This means that you could give a single column, or multiple columns separated with commas.

This notation is admittedly imprecise. There are other notations, such as Backus-Naur Form (BNF), that are much more rigorous. But they are complex and difficult to read. For our purposes here, this notation is easy, and it is precise enough.

2.3. Adventures in Real Life

Throughout the book I give examples from real companies and real systems that highlight a point being made in the main text, and that I think are interesting or amusing. Most of these are from my personal experience, though a few are from other sources.

While most of these examples highlight bad design decisions, my purpose is not to make fun of past co-workers or indulge in "I told you so"s. (Well, that's not my only purpose.) Rather, I am trying to show that the principles I discuss in this book are not hypothetical, but address real problems encountered in the real world. To be fair, I have included some examples of design decisions that I have made myself that later turned out to be dumb ideas. The fact that someone makes a mistake doesn't mean they're stupid, just that they made a mistake.

These examples are highlighted with the heading "Adventures in Real Life".

Note: In many of these stories I have changed the names of things in the computer system from specialized terms peculiar to the organization to more familiar words. There was little point in bogging down a story with an explanation of somebody's unusual jargon. So the stories are true, but the names are changed to protect the innocent.

2.4.   Naming Names

When I make up names for things that are found in a database, i.e. "database objects", I write them with the first letter of each word capitalized. For example, if I say that our example database will include a table to hold information about sales to employees, I will refer to this as the "Employee Sales" table. This helps distinguish database objects from other references.

2.5.   Punctuation

There are two competing sets of rules in the English language for the placement of quotes around punctuation: the "British system" and the "American system".

In the American system, whether punctuation goes inside or outside the quote marks depends on the kind of punctuation: for example commas and periods go inside; colons go outside. In the British system, whether a punctuation mark goes inside or outside depends on whether or not it is logically part of the quote.

The problem with the American system is that it is ambiguous.

 Adventures in Real Life!

In a users guide for a computer system, I had to explain how to enter dollar amounts. So I wrote:

Enter dollar amounts as dollars only, no cents. Do not include the dollar sign, decimal point, or commas. For example, you would enter $42.00 as "42".

Note that I used the British system: I put the period outside the quotes because it was not part of the quote. If I had used the American system I would have written

For example, you would enter $42.00 as "42."

It would surely be confusing to say that you should not include the decimal point, and then give an example that appears to include a decimal point.

The names are somewhat of a misnomer, as both systems are used in both countries, but it is true that most Americans use the American system and most Britons use the British system. Despite the fact that I am a patriotic American, I must concede that the British system is superior, and so it is what I use in this book.

I give this long explanation, not because it is a very important point, but to head off criticism from grammar legalists. It is not a mistake, but a deliberate act of rebellion.

2.6.   Review Questions

I end most chapters with a half dozen or so review questions that cover the major points from that chapter. I encourage you to try to jot down answers to these questions, or at least to formulate answers in your head. If you have difficulty doing this, perhaps your mind wandered while reading and you should go back and re-read what you missed.

3. GAME PLAN

A goal without a plan is just a wish.

-- Antoine de Saint-Exupery

3.1. The Goal

In this book I present a step-by-step plan for designing and building a database. I'll explain each step in detail in the following chapters, but it's good to have a general idea where you're going so that you can see how all the pieces fit together. In this chapter I give an overview of the steps.

Database design is a creative process. When I say that this is a step-by-step plan, I don't mean that in the sense that you might have instructions to assemble a toy or a bookcase that can be followed mindlessly. Rather, the steps are a guide to help you organize your thinking.

At the highest level, what are we trying to accomplish?

The purpose of database design is to create an information model of the subject that we want to build a computer system for. We call it a "model" because it is not reality – our database is not actually a collection of customers or students or weather phenomena or whatever – but a representation of reality, a simplification. Like a plastic model car or airplane that you might have built as a kid, a database model "looks like" the real thing in some sense, but of course it is not the real thing. It includes the points important to us for our present purposes, and ignores complexities that we don't care about right now.

Computer systems are all about information, so a database model is about information. What do we need to know about this subject? What information do we need to keep, and how can we organize it to satisfy our goals?

A database model includes those aspects of the real world that are relevant to this system. There are many things in the real world that we don't care about right now. That doesn't mean that they are not important, just that they are not important *to us*. For example, when we describe our customers, we care about things like what products they want to buy and how they intend to pay for them. The fact that Edna is a nice old lady who loves her grandchildren or that Bob gets violent when he is drunk are no doubt very important facts to these people's lives, but are not important to our computer system. (Unless we are selling Edna frames for the pictures of her grandchildren, or searching for legal precedents to keep Bob out of jail.)

3.2.   The Good Model

What makes a good model?

A database design should be judged on three criteria: accuracy, efficiency, and maintainability.

"Accuracy" means that it works, that it results in users getting the correct information. Clearly this is the most important criteria. A database that is lightning fast but consistently gives wrong answers is a bad database. Being very good at being wrong is not much of a virtue.

For a database, accuracy means that it correctly represents the information required for the subject.

"Efficiency" means that it uses a minimum of computer resources, like disk space and CPU time, and that it responds to the user quickly.

A system that gives accurate answers in 2 seconds is clearly better than a system that takes 2 minutes to give the same results. How fast is fast enough depends on the circumstances. A system that generates five-year economic forecasts for long-term planning is probably acceptable if it takes hours or even days to churn out a report. A system to intercept incoming missiles is rather useless if it gives results one second after the missile hits.

A good database uses a minimum of disk space to store its data, using a variety of techniques that will fill several chapters of this book.

Of course speed is a factor of both the database and the software that accesses it, but a well-designed database can at least make it possible for database accesses to be fast. The programmers may fail to take advantage, but that's a different issue.

"Maintainability" means that when another designer comes to make a change to this database months or years after it was originally built, he can figure out what the original designer was doing and why, and the design is flexible enough that he can make the required changes without having to re-work parts of the design that are not directly related. This criterion is often neglected. It's easy to get in a hurry to meet a deadline and throw something together that meets the immediate requirement without considering the long-term implications. But the reality is that we are going to spend a lot more time maintaining the database – making changes and updates – then we will spend building it initially. If you don't have time to do it correctly now, what makes you think you'll have time to fix it later?

Perhaps the best path to maintainability is simplicity. Computer people often praise an "elegant" design. By this we mean a design that completely solves the problem but is fundamentally simple and easy to understand, with a minimum of special cases. To a certain extent, simple means small. The fewest distinct objects in your database, the more elegant it likely is. But this principle can be applied to excess. We do not want to simplify to the point that we are no longer meeting the requirements.

3.3. Pieces of a Model

So what goes in to a model? There are four essential pieces. Let's begin with some plain English descriptions of these pieces. In later chapters I will give more technical definitions.

Entity: A class of people, places, or things that is relevant to the current problem. This may remind you of the definition for a noun that you were taught in elementary school, and indeed entities are named with nouns or noun phrases. By "noun phrase" here, I mean a noun with modifying terms, such as adjectives.

Example: If we are working on a system to record customer orders, entities might include "Customer", "Product", and "Order".

An entity is a *class* of things and not an individual thing. An individual thing is called an "entity instance", or simply an "instance". Thus, "American President" could be an entity; "Abraham Lincoln" would be an instance of this entity.

Relationship: A connection or association between two entities. Relationships are named with verbs or verb phrases.

Example: Orders may be broken into line items, so we would have the relationship "Order *has* Line Item". If we have a specific salesman assigned to each customer, we have a relationship "Salesman *is assigned to* Customer" (or "Salesman *serves* Customer" or however we choose to describe it).

Often the relationship is so obvious that giving it a distinct name is trite and wordy, and we just call it by the names of the two entities it relates. In the above example, we might talk about the "Salesman-Customer relationship" or simply "Salesman-Customer". Anyone familiar with the idea of taking orders would surely understand what this means. But if there is any doubt or ambiguity, give it a real name. For example, "Employee-Product" is probably unacceptably ambiguous. Does this mean the employee who sells the product? The employee who inspects the product? An employee who bought the product with an employee discount? Etc.

Attribute: A piece of information that we want to keep about an entity.

Example: For an Employee entity, we likely want to keep "Employee Name", "Social Security Number", "Address", and so on.

Key: One or more attributes that, when taken together, uniquely identify an entity instance.

Example: A key for "Product" might be "Catalog Number".

Note that it might require more than one attribute to make up a key. A key for "Tax Return" might be "Taxpayer ID" plus "Year". Either one by itself would be insufficient to identify a specific tax return.

We refer to all these things collectively as "database objects" or simply "objects".

3.4.   The Model Sequence

We design a database by creating a series of "models". As we progress, these models become more detailed and closer to what will actually run on the computer. When we are building our first model, we don't want to get bogged down deciding how many digits to allow for On-hand Quantity and whether Item Number should be all numeric or a mix of letters and digits before we've decided whether we want to keep product or inventory information at all.

In this book I describe a series of three models, which I call the logical model, the physical model, and the implementation. (Note on terminology: While these terms are routinely used in database theory, their exact definitions vary. For example, what I am calling a "logical model" here, others call a "conceptual model". Many like to have a name for "implementation" that includes the word "model" to make clear that it, too, is a model. So don't worry much about the names of the models, just about the concepts.)

The "logical model" is an idealized model that describes the database in terms of the real-world information that we want to hold. At this stage we will use some high-level abstractions that we know full well cannot actually be done directly in any real-world databases product. But it's easier to think of the database this way, so we describe it like this and worry about the harsh realities of life later. We don't worry about what will be efficient. We don't worry about exactly which database product we are going to use to build this database. If you find yourself saying, "I'll do it this way because that will run faster in Oracle," you're getting ahead of yourself.

With the "physical model" we give in to reality a little. Here we modify our logical model to meet the limitations of commercial database products in general and sometimes even of the specific database product that we plan to use. Now is the time to start thinking about what will work well, or work at all.

The "implementation" is the set of commands or statements in a specific database product to create a real database from the model. That is, an implementation is a set of SQL statements, or a set of screens where we enter detailed information necessary to allocate space on a hard drive and create the appropriate files that a program can actually use. You might consider the SQL the "real thing" because it is used to directly create a real database, or you might consider it to be a third-level model, because SQL statements are not the actual database files and the database is not the reality. In this book I'll call it a model for the convenience of being able to talk about "the three models" rather than "the two models and that other thing".

In a very important sense, we might use not three models, but dozens. We build each model in steps, and it could be argued that each of these steps is really a different model. But that would be a boring argument: Call it what you want, as long as we all know what we're talking about.

Furthermore, we almost never create any of these models in their final form on the first try. In real life we start with incomplete information, we make mistakes, we get better ideas as we go along, etc. We normally go through many drafts before we get a version that we are happy with.

3.5.   Steps

So here are the steps we are going to follow:

1: Build the logical model. A "logical model" is a description of the database that emphasizes the real-world things that it is about. To build the logical model, we go through three sub-steps:
1.1. Identify the entities.
1.2. Identify the relationships between the entities.
1.3. Identify the attributes and assign attributes to entities.
2. Build a physical model from the logical model. The physical model is an adjustment of the logical model that allows for limitations of present database technology.
2.1. Implement entities as tables.
2.2. Implement relationships with posted identifiers and indexes.
2.3. Promote many-to-many relationships to tables
2.4. Add lookup lists and other "convenience tables".
2.5. "Normalize" the tables. This is a process for weeding out redundant and ambiguous data. But sometimes the rulebook gets us into trouble, so we have to "denormalize".

3. Implement the physical model with a real database product. Turn the model into a system that can run on a real computer.

3.1. Translate the model to SQL or whatever database language we are using

3.2. Create indexes, sequences, and other practicalities.

3.3. Deploy! You're done! At least until your users have changes.

You should generally follow the steps in the order listed. Of course in real life you will often discover that you have made a mistake and have to go back to an earlier step. You may get new information that requires you to rework something. You will surely have later steps in mind as you do earlier steps. If you get a brainstorm about how to do something in step 3.2 in a particularly clever way while you are "officially" working on step 2.3, there's no harm in writing this down before you forget.

But you should try to stay basically on track. Running all over the place working on whatever strikes your fancy at the moment is likely to lead to forgetting things and half-done jobs.

3.6.   What Does a Model Look Like?

Both the logical and physical models are diagrams, charts, or other convenient representations. They are normally visual and graphical.

Perhaps the simplest form of logical or physical model is the "Entity Attribute List", or EAL. This is simply a list of entities with associated attributes.

A Data Dictionary is an exhaustive list of all the attributes with names, definitions, formats, and anything else we know about them.

The most common and valuable representation is the Entity-Relationship Diagram, or ERD. This is a drawing with boxes for entities and lines to show their relationships. Symbols on the lines give information about the nature of the relationship. Usually we do not mention attributes in an ERD, though we can write them in. If you are designing a database, you will spend much or your life drawing and updating ERDs.

In the old days database designers drew these diagrams on paper or on a chalkboard, and there was no way to create a database directly from such models. Today there are software products that can be used to draw these diagrams on the computer, and then allow the database designer to later add in additional detail, and the software product generates the SQL statements or the equivalent. The fact that you may be able to create all three models with one tool does not have anything to do with the differences between them. I can use Microsoft Word to write a novel and also to create a spreadsheet. That doesn't mean that a spreadsheet is a novel. It just means that MS Word has a variety of features.

The logical and physical models have a similar "look". That is, we use the same sort of diagrams and charts to depict them. In a very simple database they might be identical. It's possible that the real-world situation that we want to describe with our database just happens to be easy to build with a commercial database product. Possible, but rare.

An implementation is, by definition, written in the language of a particular database product. Therefore, what it looks like depends on the database product you are using. Most database products today use Structured Query Language, or SQL, so that is what I will use in this book. They each have their own dialect of SQL, of course, because it would make things much too easy on database designers if they were all the same. But I will use very generic SQL examples here that should work with a large variety of database products.

The SQL statements that make up an implementation are primarily "create table" statements. These name a table (i.e. entity), list the columns (i.e. attributes) that make up that table, and give various other information about the columns and the table as a whole. We'll discuss SQL further in chapter 5. But for example:

```
create table customer_order (order_number
numeric(10), customer_number numeric(10),
order_date date,shipping_method char(2),
primary key (order_number))
```

This creates a table (entity) named "customer_order" with four columns (attributes): order_number, customer_number, order_date, and shipping_method. order_number and customer_number are numbers with a maximum of 10 digits; order_date is a date (duh), and shipping_method is a character string with exactly 2 characters. The primary key (identifier) is order_number.

3.7. Permanence of the Logical Model

Some experts make much of the claim that a logical model is "permanent". That is, they explain, once you have a valid logical model, as long as your organization does not change, the model should never change.

This may be true but by the time you think through what it means, it is not very interesting. It is only valid if we understand it to mean that as long as absolutely nothing about your organization changes, the logical model should not change. But suppose you take on new activities, like, you used to make dress shoes, but now you have decided to also make sneakers. Your organization has changed, you have taken on new activities, so the logical model may change. Or you used to group your offices into regions, but now you group them into districts within regions. Your organization has changed, so the logical model may change.

The logical model could be permanent in the sense that if your database hardware or software changes, the logical model should not change. But even that is debatable: As the technology advances, surely we will conclude that things we were doing with logical models yesterday are out of date.

So I wouldn't worry much about the permanence idea.

3.8.   Programming

Of course database design is only part of a software project. Another obvious piece is programming. A database with no software to access it is not going to be very useful to your users.

Good database design is more important than good programming. I am both a programmer and a database designer, so I do not say this to denigrate programmers. But if a program is poorly written, we can usually fix the problem by fixing that one program. If necessary we can throw it out and rewrite it. If any part of a database is poorly designed, fixing it can be a major effort. Once programming begins, there will quickly be dozens, maybe even hundreds, of programs that are written based on that database design. Fixing the database will require making changes to all of those programs. In real life, the effort and risk involved in making so many changes will often just be too large, and we will have no choice but to live with the bad database.

As this is a book about database design and not about programming – let's not bite off more than we can chew! – for the rest of this book I will only mention programming incidentally.

3.9.   Players

There are several different roles involved in designing a database.

User: Someone who will ultimately be using the database that we create, or a supervisor over such people. Usually these are people who are doing the job now, either manually, with ad hoc systems like word processors and spreadsheets, or with an older computer system that we will replace, called a "legacy system". A user is generally expected to know what needs to be accomplished in the real world. Of course the user may or may not know anything about designing computer systems. A user should be an expert on the business area (or government or academic or whatever), not on computers.

Business analyst: Translates the business requirements into computer terms. A business analyst does not have to know about programming or database administration. He just has to know in general terms what computer systems are capable of.

Database designer: Understands databases and can relate business requirements to what can actually be done with a database. Some consider a database designer to be a special kind of business analyst; others see business analysts as less technical and database designers as more technical.

Database administrator: Someone skilled in constructing, configuring, tuning, and maintaining a database on a computer using a real-world database product. A database administrator is a highly technical person, skilled in the use of specific database products.

Programmer: Writes software to make the computer perform the desired operations. In a database system, this includes telling the computer when and how to retrieve information from the database and what to do with it.

On large projects, there may be many people in each of these roles.

On small projects, one person might perform several of these roles, maybe even all of them. The database designer may also be the database administrator and the programmer. When a computer person works for the same organization for a long time, he often becomes very knowledgeable about the organization's processes, so the database analyst may know enough to function as a user. Etc.

3.10.   Review Questions

1. Why do we call a database a "model"?

2. What are the pieces that make up a database model?

3. List the three models and explain the differences between them.

4. What are the steps to building a database?

5. Who is involved in designing and building a database?

4. TERMINOLOGY

[U]nless you utter by the tongue words easy to understand, how will it be known what is spoken? For you will be speaking into the air.

-- 1 Corinthians 14:9 (NKJV)

4.1. General

A good first step in communicating is to speak the same language. So let's begin by defining some basic terms.

There are some terms in the "database world" that have standard definitions that are widely used and understood. In this book, I define these and I have tried to use them in the accepted sense. There are other terms that are not so standard, or ideas for which there is no widely-recognized term. When I use one of these, I state that this is not a universal term. Hopefully this will help avoid confusion when you talk to other database people.

Many of these terms are used in general, vague ways, even among computer people. In this book I try to give them precise definitions and to stick to those definitions.

Database engine: A software tool that controls access to data, providing some sort of indexed random access, ways to relate data, and ways to dynamically modify the structure of the data. Also called a "database management system" or DBMS.

Database product: A database engine made by a particular company or organization. (Normally we are thinking of a commercial product like Oracle or MySQL, but this term also includes open source products like Postgres, etc.) Of course every database engine must be made by *somebody*, but I use the term "database product" when I want to make clear that one brand may be different from another.

Database: A collection of data accessed through a database engine.

Schema: A description of the layout and structure of a particular database.

People often use the term "database" to refer both to a specific collection of data, and to the engine that provides access to that data. In this book I clearly distinguish the two as a "database" versus a "database engine".

Note that a database engine is a generic tool. Typically an organization will buy one database engine and use it for many different databases. (They may buy many copies to spread the workload across many computers, but they are using the same product.) Many organizations will buy and use the same database engine. A database, on the other hand, is typically built for one organization, and for just one project or set of related projects. "Oracle" is a database engine. "My company's employee data" is a database.

Note: The SQL standard defines a schema as a subset of a database. The more traditional database terminology defined each database as having exactly one schema. If it was necessary to talk about a specific portion of the database, we would call it a "sub-schema". In this book I will talk about a database as having a single schema. The SQL definition makes sense from the point of view of the builders of a database product because it is possible to physically store more than one schema in the same "place", and the database engine needs a name for that place, so they call it a "database". But logically, each schema is a separate database, they just happened to be living together. It's like the difference between a room mate and a family member.

4.2. Database Objects

Here I must admit that when it comes to discussing databases, there are many cases where we use terms interchangeably, that is, where we use several different words for essentially the same idea. Partly this is because there are subtle technical distinctions. Mostly it is because many people have contributed to the art of database design, and as each thinker wrote a book on his ideas, he found it necessary to make up new words for all the old concepts.

There are three commonly-used sets of terms for the things that make up a database: I will call these the "file system" set, the "database theory" set, and the "relational" or "SQL" set. As follows:

	File System	Database	Relational
A single piece of information	Field	Attribute	Column
A set of fields (etc) about the same individual person, place, or thing	Record	Entity Instance, Tuple, Relation	Row
A group of related records (etc)	File	Entity	Table
Something that identifies a record (etc)	Key	Identifier	Key

Note that in the relational terminology, a table is made up of rows and columns. This is intended to bring to mind a table or chart that you might draw on a piece of paper.

There are some technical distinctions between these terms, but they are largely synonymous.

Technically, a "table" can be either an "entity" or a "relationship", as I shall explain in chapter 12, Physical Model.

We normally talk about an entity having only one identifier, but a file or table can have many keys. A closer synonym to identifier is "primary key".

Database designers often use the word "file" as a synonym for "entity" and "table". But "file" also has a specific meaning to the operating system: it is a collection of data that the OS manages and manipulates as a unit. A database engine may store many tables in a single OS file, or it may break a single table across multiple OS files. In practice this rarely causes confusion: When we're talking about a logical or a physical model and use the word "file", we almost surely mean the same thing as "entity". When a database administrator is talking about configuring and tuning the database, he will use "file" to mean "OS file" and "table" to mean "table".

All of these things are collectively referred to as "objects". That is, any kind of thing that goes into our database is an object.

In this book, I use the terms "entity" and "attribute" when discussing the logical model – which is the bulk of the book – and "table" and "column" when discussing the physical model, and the implementation and SQL. I do this simply to bow to the conventions of the database world. Entity-Relationship Diagrams are well known by that name, and for me to suddenly start calling them "Table Relationship Diagrams" would be confusing to anyone who ever has or will read any other database books. Likewise, I don't think the national and international standards committees are going to re-write SQL at this point to revise the terminology.

I use the word "record" throughout. "Entity instance" is awkward and is often confused with "entity", so I avoid it except when it is necessary to emphasize the idea that something is an instance of a particular entity. "Relation" sounds too much like "relationship", which is a completely different concept. "Row" sounds too generic.

I use the word "key" throughout.

I do not use the words "field", "file", or "tuple" in this book. They're perfectly good words and I routinely use them elsewhere, but for the sake of consistency I avoid them here.

4.3. Types of Databases

This book is all about designing "relational databases". This is a distinction that is barely necessary to state, because almost all databases today are relational databases.

There were other kinds of databases in the past, but they are almost extinct. There are new kinds of databases being experimented with, but to the best of my knowledge, none has yet been commercially successful.

The earliest databases were "network" or "hierarchical". In a network database, the linkages between entities were determined at the time the database was built. Connections were implemented with record numbers or disk locations. So if at the time the database was designed the designer included a linkage between, say, Customer and Order, then queries and programs could easily find all the orders for a customer. But if no linkage was made between Customer and State, like for his state of residence, then queries could not make this connection at all and programs had to go to extra steps. A hierarchical database was even more limited in that each entity could have only one linkage. Thus databases had to be built in a hierarchy, like a business organization chart, where you could trace up or down the levels.

In a relational database, linkages are not predefined. Linkages are made "on the fly" based on data. If a Customer entity has an attribute for State Abbreviation, and our State entity has an attribute for State Abbreviation, then we can easily find the State information for this Customer or all the Customers in this State with a single query. We can use more complex operations to "join" tables in ways that the database designer may never have considered.

Relational databases are sometimes called RDBs for short.

A new idea in databases is the Object-Oriented Database, or OODB. The main difference between an RDB and an OODB is that an OODB has the concept of "sub-types". Suppose our company has employees. We keep information about these employees like their names, hire dates, and departments. Some employees are salesmen, others are factory workers, others are engineers, etc. For each type, we have information we want to keep specific to that type. Salesmen have quotas and assigned regions. Factory workers are skilled on various machines. Engineers are assigned to specific development projects. Etc. It doesn't make sense to talk about the sales quota of an engineer or the machine skills of a salesman. But all employees have a name and a hire date. An OODB creates types and sub-types, so we can describe the common information in the type and the different information in the sub-type. An RDB does not have this concept. If we have different kinds of employees, we either create separates entities for each of them, in which case common information is described multiple times and common processes must go against multiple entities, or we put them in a single entity and much of the data is inapplicable in any given case.

But there are a lot of problems in making an OODB a practical commercial product. Perhaps someday OODBs will take over the database world. Or perhaps they will prove to be a blind alley. Right now, they're not where the database world is, so I will not be discussing them further in this book.

Another new idea is XML databases. These are databases based on the eXtended Markup Language, which is a language originally developed for describing text documents. These support extremely complex structures: entities nested inside other entities in many possible combinations. Supporters of this idea say that this makes them extremely flexible. Skeptics say it makes them extremely complicated with little apparent benefit. I won't discuss these any further here, either.

4.4. Review Questions

1. What is the difference between a "database" and a "database engine"?

2. List the three sets of terms for database objects. Discuss the parallels and differences between them.

3. What are the five types of database discussed in this chapter? What are the differences between them? Which are we going to be working with?

5. INTRODUCTION TO SQL

Could life so end, half told; its school so fail?
Soul, soul, there is a sequel to thy tale!

--Robert Mowry Bell

5.1. Disclaimer

In this book I use SQL when concrete examples are appropriate. SQL is the most popular language for database engines today, so it is a logical choice.

The "official" pronunciation of SQL is "ess que el", that is, you are supposed to say the names of the letters. But the original version was called "Sequel" and many people pronounce it "sequel".

SQL stands for "Structured Query Language". This name is something of a misnomer as SQL can express more than simply queries.

In this chapter I try to give you the essentials of SQL. This is not a complete description of all the features of SQL. It is not intended to teach you all you need to know to use SQL in your system development. It is intended to give you an idea of what SQL can do and to teach you enough to get you through the examples in this book and to be able to talk intelligently to other people involved in a database project. All the statements I describe here have many more options that I just won't get into.

If you are already comfortable with SQL, feel free to skim this chapter or skip it completely. If you are not comfortable with SQL and will be interacting with the database directly – creating databases or writing programs -- I strongly encourage you to get a book devoted to the subject, or to read the documentation that comes with your database product, before attempting to implement a database. If you are an analyst or designer who won't be doing any actual programming, this chapter should be sufficient.

The examples in this book were all tested with mySQL version 4.1.22. Exceptions are noted.

5.2.   Building Blocks

First you should understand some of the building blocks that go into larger SQL statements: data types, identifiers, and expressions.

5.2.1. Data Types

The most important data types in SQL are:

char(n)	A character string consisting of exactly "n" characters. This will be filled out with spaces if you give a value that is shorter.
varchar(n)	A variable number of characters, up to "n".
numeric(n)	An integer of up to "n" digits. This may be positive or negative. Depending on the database product, "n" may or may include the space required for a minus sign.
decimal(n,m)	A number with up to "n" digits, including "m" digits after the decimal point.
int	An integer in the "natural size" of the computer. Most database products store int's as 4-byte binary, but this is not universal.
float	A floating point number in the natural size and format of the computer.
date	A calendar date, at least allowing all dates from AD 0 to AD 9999.
time	A time of day, without a date.
timestamp	Date and time. Often this is a fairly high precision, like to the millisecond.

The SQL standard defines a number of other data types, and many database products have their own custom types.

A depressing reality is that the implementation of these data types is very inconsistent. The size of an "int" varies. Some database products include the time of day in a "date" column. The maximum size that can be given for the types with lengths, like "varchar" and "number", varies. Etc.

Handling of Booleans is particularly inconsistent between SQL engines. A "Boolean" -- or "logical" -- value is true or false. (Or null, as we shall get to shortly.) Some SQL engines have an explicit Boolean data type. In others you have to fake it. You can create a char(1) and give it values of "T" or "F", or an integer and use zero for false and one for true. Database vendors often encourage one way or another to "simulate" Booleans.

Read the documentation that comes with your database product to see the definitions.

5.2.2. Constants

Numeric constants are written as a string of digits. You may write a sign in front of the digits. If the number type allows decimals, you may include a decimal point.

Examples:

```
17
-37
28.4
```

Character constants must be enclosed in single quotes. If the constant includes a quote mark, it must be doubled.

Examples:

```
'My text'
'O''Reilly'
```

Note that you must use single quotes, not double quotes.

According to the standard, date constants are written as year, hyphen, month, hyphen, day, enclosed in quotes. The year must be four digits and the month and day two each.

Example:

```
'1945-08-06'
```

Times are written as hours, colon, minutes, colon, seconds.
Example:

```
'11:28:30'
```

Timestamps are written as a date, a space, and a time.
Example:

```
'1945-08-06 11:28:30'
```

However, some SQL engines use other date and time formats.

According to the standard, Boolean constants are "true" and "false". Support for these values is very uneven.

5.2.3. Nulls

Every data type in SQL allows the special value of "null". Null means "not specified" or "unknown". Many pre-SQL database systems did not have such a feature, and so the system would store blank or zero when the value was unknown. This creates all sorts of problems. Suppose we are building a system for a bank. When someone applies for a loan, we do a credit check under both the husband's and the wife's names. If at the time that our clerk is filling in the screen, she does not know the customer's spouse's name, she leaves it blank. But how do we then know if blank means that we just haven't got this information yet, or that the customer is not married?

Adventures
in Real Life!

There was a rather famous case where the inability to distinguish blank from unknown caused amusing results. When the police in California write a parking ticket, there is a box on the form for "License plate number". But what if the car does not have a valid license plate? This would, of course, be reason of itself for giving someone a ticket. So in that case the policeman simply wrote in "None" or similar words, and these were duly entered into the computer.

Then a Los Angeles man got the license number "NO PLATE" due to a mistake in the paperwork for a personalized plate. He decided to keep it because he found it amusing. But when the motor vehicle department's computer system next processed tickets, it found lots of overdue tickets with this license number for which it had not previously been able to find an address. Over the course of the next few months this unfortunate man was sent over 2,000 parking tickets from all over the state!

(http://www.snopes.com/autos/law/noplate.asp)

Clearly, there is a big difference between no plate and a license number of "NO PLATE".

We sometimes use the Greek small letter omega, "ω", to represent null. This avoids some possible confusion: If we use blank for null, does that mean null or does it mean a string of zero characters? The two are not the same to the database engine. (Oracle treats them as the same, but it is the only database product I know of that does this.) We could use the word "null", but again, does that mean null or does it mean the four letters "n", "u", "l", "l"? I once had a maddening problem where a column was set equal to the four letters "null". When I printed the record, it said "null", which I assumed meant the column was null. But then when I compared it to null, the result was false. I spent quite a while circling around before I figured out what the problem was.

Unfortunately, a small omega looks a lot like a small double-u in many fonts, so this convention may just replace one ambiguity with another. (And it's ethnocentric: It does nothing to eliminate ambiguity for Greek-speaking people.) I often use the omega in handwritten papers where I can exaggerate the loops so it doesn't look like any English letter, but I won't be using that notation in this book.

Of course the user usually does not understand the concept of a null, so we typically display it as blank.

5.2.4. Identifiers

In SQL, an "identifier" is a name for a database object: a table, column, etc. (Note that a SQL "identifier" is not the same thing as an "identifier" in database theory. As I mentioned in chapter 4, in database theory an identifier is one or more attributes that uniquely identify a record. So we have one word that means two very different things. Hopefully the meaning will be clear from the context.)

All names must follow the same basic rules. They normally can include only letters, digits, and underscores. A name cannot begin with a digit. The maximum length of a name varies between database products, but is usually at least 16. A SQL keyword cannot be used as a name. For example, you cannot create a table named "table" or a column named "group", because "table" and "group" are words with special meaning to SQL.

Some database products allow additional special characters in a name. Some allow you to use any character you like or to use key words as long as you put the name in quotes. In general I'd discourage you from doing this, as it gets confusing.

Names are not case-sensitive, and internally are often translated to all capitals. If you are a C or Java programmer, you may be used to writing names in "camelCase", that is, running words together using a capital for the first letter of each word to break them up, like "CustomerOrderStatus". This doesn't work in SQL. It will come out as "CUSTOMERORDERSTATUS", which can be hard to read. Either use recognizable abbreviations to make the names very short, or use underscores to separate the words, like "ordstatus" or "customer_order_status".

It is sometimes annoying when the obvious name for something is a key word. Like if you have an order processing system, you may well want to call the table that holds the orders, "order". Unfortunately that's a key word used to specify sorting. One solution in these cases is to add an additional word or words to make it distinct. You might call it "customer_order". Another option is to deliberately misspell the word. I routinely use the name "uzer" for a table of registered users. Or you could just think of another name.

5.2.5. Expressions

If you've done any programming, SQL expressions will seem quite familiar to you. The rules are pretty much the same as in C, Java, Visual Basic, etc.

If you've never done any programming, SQL expressions resemble the expressions you learned in algebra. Important differences are: Variable names are normally full words or phrases rather than a single letter. While we use the conventional "+" for plus and "-" for minus, we use "*" for times and "/" for divided by. Rather than write fractions with a top and bottom we separate the numerator and denominator with a divided-by symbol ("/"); if necessary we put parentheses around each part. When we need groupings within grouping, we use parentheses for all of them rather than brackets and braces. The computer and the human reader must match up parentheses by counting levels.

If you've never done any programming and never learned any algebra or don't remember it, you probably should study at least the basics before trying to go very far with computers.

In SQL there are four kinds of expressions: numeric, character, date, and logical. Numeric, character, and date expressions are used when assigning values. In some SQL database engines, logical expressions can only be used when testing conditions, that is, they cannot be used to calculate and save a Boolean value. Other database products are more flexible and allow Boolean assignment.

An arithmetic expression is about what you would expect: You can use the basic arithmetic operations – plus (+), minus (-), times (*), and divided by (/) – on numeric columns and/or constants. Parentheses can be used to force operations to be done in the desired order.

Example:

```
x+y*(c-4)/3
```

There is also a collection of functions that operate on numbers. I won't get into those here.

A character expression works on character columns or constants. Most versions of SQL have a character concatenation operator, '| |', to combine two character values. Thus:

```
'Hello' || ', ' || 'world'
```

gives the result

```
'Hello, world'
```

Besides that all character operations are functions. Perhaps the most commonly-used function is "substring", which extracts a portion of a character string. It is written as

```
substring(bigstring from start for length)
```

Example:

```
substring('Happiness' from 4 for 3)
```

This extracts a piece of a character string, namely the piece beginning at "from" for a length of "for". The first position is "1". (Unlike some programming languages, where we start counting from zero.)
The above example gives:

```
'pin'
```

Many database products allow this to be cast in the more compact and conventional style:

```
substring(bigstring, start, length)
```

So the above example would become

```
substring('Happiness',4,3)
```

Other commonly-used functions are "upper" and "lower", which convert characters to all upper or all lower case; and "trim", which removes leading and/or trailing spaces.

There are many other functions, and they vary between database products. Consult your documentation.

A date expression works on dates and intervals between dates. When discussing SQL expressions, we use the term "date" to include times and timestamps.

According to the standard, you can add an integer to a date. A positive number means that many days toward the future; a negative number means that many days toward the past. For example, '1941-12-07' + 30 gives '1942-01-06'.

You can subtract one date from another to get the number of days between them.

This doesn't work in all versions of SQL. (This did not work for me in mySQL but did work in Postgres.)

You can never add two dates together because this does not make sense.

A logical expression is a comparison of number, character, and/or date expressions, or several such comparisons linked together with "and" and "or". It returns a Boolean.

Comparison operators are equals (=), not equal (!= or <>), less than (<), less than or equal (<=), greater than (>), and greater than or equal (>=). (Note that the equality comparison operator is a single equal sign, not a double equals as in some programming languages.)

When used on numbers, these give the results you learned in third grade.

When used on dates, they reflect chronological order. '1961-04-12' < '1969-07-20' is true.

When used on characters, they reflect alphabetical order, for example, 'A'<'B'. And from there things get a little more complicated. Comparisons between letters and digits and between upper and lower case depend on the character set. (Or more technically, on the "collating sequence".) With standard Latin1, all upper case letters are less than lower case letters. Digits are less than any letter. Most punctuation is less than digits.

So '*'<'0'<'9'<'A'<'Z'<'a'<'z'.

(In mySQL, character comparisons are case insensitive, so 'A'='a', etc. In Oracle and Postgres, 'A'<'a'.)

Remember that when comparing characters, even if a character string contains digits it is compared by alphabetical order, not as a number. For example, while the number 19>2, the character string '19'<'2', because '1' is less than '2' alphabetically, so we never look past that.

Another character comparison operator is "like". This compares a character string to a pattern. The pattern can include ordinary characters and "wildcards". There are two wildcards. An underscore (_) matches any one character. A percent (%) matches any string of characters. Anything else is taken literally.

Examples:

'Mary' like 'Mar_' is true. The '_' matches the 'y'. Note this pattern would also match 'Mare' and 'Mark'.

'Mary' like 'Ma_' is false. The '_' matches the 'r' but then there is no match for the 'y'.

'Mary' like 'M%y' is true. The '%' matches 'ar'. This pattern would also match 'May' and 'Manifold is the story'. Spaces are treated like any other character for matching purposes.

'Mary' like 'Mar%y' is true. The '%' matches the empty string.

Watch for unexpected matches. Suppose you are searching a list of products for service fees. So you search for '%fee%'. This matches 'restocking fee' and 'fee for special orders' and anything else with the word 'fee' in it, so that might look good. But it also matches 'coffee table' and 'bird feeder'.

Some database engines include the "similar to" operator, which allows more complex pattern matching.

Any comparison against a null value gives a result of neither true nor false, but null, i.e. unknown. The idea is that if x is unknown, then comparing x to anything gives an unknown result. This applies to all types of compares.

"null=null" is not true but null. The idea is that unknown compared to another unknown is always unknown – there's no reason to believe that two unknowns are equal to each other. If we want to check if something is null, we have to use a special construct, "is null". As in, "x is null" rather than "x=null".

Logical operations are a little more complicated. "x and y" is true only if both x and y are true. So "false and null" is false, because it wouldn't matter what was in the second position, the result would still be false. But "true and null" is null, because the result depends on the second value. Similarly, "x or y" is true if either x or y is true. So "true or null" is true, but "false or null" is null, by similar reasoning.

Note that a single null value in an expression can ripple all the way through. Consider

```
price+tax>1000.00 and state='KY'
```

If state is null, then the whole expression is null. That may be obvious from what I've just said. What may be not so obvious is that if tax is null, then price+tax is null, so price+tax>1000 is null, so the whole expression is null. Even if price by itself is over 1000, price+tax>1000 will still be null. As a human you may realize that it doesn't mater what the tax is if the price is already over 1000, but SQL doesn't know that the tax won't be negative.

When an action is dependent on a logical expression and the final value is null, this is treated as false.

(While most database designers agree that the introduction of nulls was a brilliant innovation in SQL, the details of its handling do get awkward in many cases. Some database designers and programmers complain that it was poorly implemented. But our purpose here is not to brainstorm features for a better database language but to understand SQL as it is.)

5.3. The Two SQLs

There are two major pieces to SQL: The Data Definition Language, or DDL, and the Data Manipulation Language, or DML.

DDL is used to create new databases and modify the schema (i.e. structure) of existing ones.

DML is used to add, change, and retrieve data from a database.

You may want to refer back to chapter 2, Style Conventions, before reading the next section.

Line breaks are normally ignored by SQL. Wherever one space is allowed or required, extra spaces are ignored. Spaces before or after punctuation, like commas and parentheses, are ignored.

In some contexts a SQL statement must be terminated by a semi-colon. I do not include the semi-colon in the examples in this chapter.

5.4. Data Definition Language

5.4.1. Create

You create a table with the SQL "create table" statement.
At its simplest, the format is:

```
create table tablename (columnname datatype, ...)
```

For example, a system for a bank might have a table for customer accounts:

```
create table account
(account_number varchar(10),
first_name varchar (20),
last_name varchar(30),
account_type char(1),
balance decimal(9,2),
last_transaction date)
```

This creates a table named "account" with columns for account_number, customer_name, and so on. account_number is a character column of varying length up to a maximum of 30, balance is a decimal number with 9 total digits including 2 after the decimal, and last_transaction is a date.

After the data type, you may optionally specify "not null", to say that this column can never contain nulls. For example:

```
create table event
(event_id int,
event_time timestamp not null)
```

As every data type allows nulls by default, any data type can be specified as "not null".

You should generally also create a primary key. (I'll have lots more on this in future chapters.) The primary key is expressed as a list of columns making up the key in parentheses and separated by commas. Like this:

```
alter table account
add primary key (account_number)
```

We'll be discussing table definition further in chapter 11, Physical Model.

5.4.2. Foreign Keys

It is often necessary for a record in one table to refer to a record in another. We call the record that is doing the referring the "child record", and the record that is referenced the "parent record". To make the reference, we include one or more columns in the child record to hold the key of the parent record. This is called a "foreign key". By "foreign" here we mean that it is a key from another table. (We'll discuss when and why we want to do this in section 12.3 and following, on realizing relationships.)

Adding the foreign key column(s) is all that is strictly necessary to make foreign keys work. One of the very useful features of relational databases is that we do not need to establish any relationships in advance: they can be made on the fly when we need them.

An inherent problem of foreign keys is that we want to make sure that the record that the foreign key refers to actually exists. That is, if an Order record is supposed to refer to a Customer record, and the Order has a foreign key referencing Customer #1297, it would be nice if there really is a customer 1297 and if this is the correct Customer.

This is called, "referential integrity". When a foreign key points to the wrong place or to a non-existent place, this is called a "corrupt foreign key".

SQL provides some features to help manage foreign keys.

The first step is to declare the foreign key. We do this by adding a "foreign key constraint". For example, suppose we have a customer_order table with the customer_number included as a foreign key to link to the customer.

```
alter table customer_order
add foreign key (customer_number)
references customer (customer_number)
```

This limits the legal values for the foreign key to values that exist as the primary key of the parent table. Unless we explicitly prohibit nulls, any foreign key column can also contain null to indicate that it has no parent. Depending on the nature of the relationship, pointing nowhere may or may not be valid. If the column was marked "not null", then it must point to some existing record. In this example, we cannot create a customer_order record with a value in customer_number that does not appear in customer.customer_number. If, say, we are just creating this database, and the only customer_number is 17, then we could create a customer_order for customer_number 17, but not for 16 or 42 or any other number. Any attempt to do so will generate an error message and the customer_order record will not be added. So in our programs, we must always add the customer record first, and then add the customer_order record.

Normally a foreign key will reference the primary key of another record, but this is not a requirement of SQL. It can reference any column in the parent table. Some database products require that this field be indexed (see next section). If it is not already indexed, declaring the foreign key will usually implicitly create an index for it.

Once we have created the customer_order record, if we try to delete the customer record, this will give an error message and the delete will not be allowed. So in our programs, if we want to delete a customer, we must first delete any customer_order records, and then delete the customer record.

Likewise, we cannot change the customer number of a customer record if there are any linked customer_order records, because this would break the link. This creates a bit of a catch-22: We cannot change the customer number of the customer_order records until we have a customer record with the new value, but we cannot change the value in the customer record as long as we have any customer_order records

There are basically four approaches to this problem.

One, some experts say that this is a moot point because you should never change the value of a primary key. This problem is one of the reasons for this convention.

Two, we could simply not tell SQL about the foreign key. Then we can manipulate it all we like, and it's up to the programmers to keep it straight. This puts the burden on the code rather than building it into the database. The advantage is that it gives us maximum flexibility. The disadvantage is that that flexibility means that we can shoot ourselves in the foot. When the database engine controls the foreign keys, we tell it the rules in one place and the engine enforces them consistently, so we can be confidant that they will always be valid. When we do it in code, we could have dozens or hundreds of programs that update this table, and if any one of them has a mistake, we could end up with corrupt foreign keys.

Three, create a new customer record with the new key value, copy all the data, change the customer_order records to point to the new customer record, and then delete the old customer record. Just from that description I think you can see that this is awkward, but certainly not impossible.

Four, some database engines offer additional features to handle deletes and/or updates automatically for us.

To use this, there are two additional clauses on the "foreign key" statement, "on delete" and "on update". For each, you can specify "restrict", "set null", or "cascade".

"on delete restrict" means to not allow the related record to be deleted when there are foreign keys pointing to it. This is the same as if the "on delete" clause is not used at all.

Similarly, "on update restrict" means to not allow the primary key to be changed if it is referenced by foreign keys, which is again the default.

"on delete set null" means that if a parent record is deleted, the foreign key in any child record is set to null.

"on update set null" means that if a parent's key is changed, the foreign key in any child is set to null.

That is, "set null" means that if the link is no longer valid, we just cut the child loose.

The real magic is when you use "cascade". "on delete cascade" means that if the parent record is deleted, all its child records are also deleted.

"on update cascade" means that if the key in the parent record is updated, then any foreign keys in child records are changed to match.

Note that not all SQL database engines support "on delete" and "on update". Some support only "on delete"; some support neither. Also note that we do not have to declare a column to be a foreign key in order to use it as a foreign key, i.e. to link two tables. Declaring it just tells the database engine to prevent it from being corrupted.

5.5. Data Manipulation Language

There are three statements for adding or changing data – insert, delete, and update -- and one (complicated) statement for retrieving and displaying data – select.

5.5.1. Insert

"insert" is used to add records to a table. The general format is:

```
insert into table (columnname,…) values
(value,…)
```

Values are constants of the appropriate type. They can also be sub-queries, which are beyond the scope of this book.
Example:

```
insert into account
(account_number, first_name, last_name,
balance)
values ('BR143-6', 'Fred', 'Stover', 147.23)
```

Alternatively, you can use the result of a select as the data for an insert:

```
insert into table
select columns, … from table where condition
```

We'll get into the format of a select in section 5.5.4. For now, just accept that select retrieves data from one or more existing tables.
Example:

```
insert into account
(account_number, first_name, last_name,
balance)
select nextval(accountseq), first_name,
last_name, 0.00
from prospect where ready_to_buy='T'
```

(mySQL did not support the nextval function. It has its own scheme for managing sequences.)

5.5.2. Delete

"delete" is used to delete records. The general format is:

```
delete from table where condition
```

'Condition' is a logical expression.
Example:

```
delete from account where
account_number='BR143-6'
```

or

```
delete from account
where last_transaction<'2001-01-01'
and account_type='W'
```

By the way, "delete" with no "where" clause means to delete all the records in the table. Be careful not to hit any "submit" key before typing in the "where" clause!

5.5.3. Update

"update" is used to change existing records. General format:

```
update table set column=value, ... where
condition
```

Example:

```
update account
set first_name='Ferd',
last_name='Stiver'
where account_number='BR143-6'
```

There are basically two ways that "where" clauses are used in "update". The syntax is the same; the difference is the practical implications.

One way is to identify a specific record. In this case the "where" clause identifies specific values for the column or columns that make up the primary key, or some other column or combination of columns that uniquely identify a record. The above example is this kind of update.

The other way is to identify a set of records that meet some condition. In this case we are not normally checking the primary key, but some more general condition.

For example, suppose we want to give every customer who has an account type of "R" and a positive balance a $5 promotional credit. We might write:

```
update account set balance=balance+5.00 where
account_type='R' and balance>0.00
```

As this example illustrates, a "set" clause can set a column to an expression rather than a simple value. This expression can involve constants and columns in the table being updated. Tutorials on SQL routinely give examples like "give everyone in department such-and-such a 10% pay raise" or like my example above, give everyone with a certain account type a credit. How often does your company give everyone in the department the same raise or every customer in some category a credit? I'm guessing jut about never. This is great for textbook examples but update is rarely used this way in real programs.

What we do routinely want to do is update one table based on another. Like, we might have a transaction file with records for all deposits and withdrawals and we want to update the balance in the customer table based on these transactions. This requires the use of sub-queries. Sub-queries are beyond the scope of this book.

5.5.4. Select

"select" is used to retrieve data from the database. It has lots of options and complexities.

The simplest form of "select" is:

```
select column, … from table where condition
```

"condition" is a logical expression.

This displays the specified column values from the specified table for all records where the condition is true.

Example:

```
select account_number, last_name, first_name
from customer where last_name='Smith'
```

This would produce something like:

ACCOUNT NUMBER	LAST NAME	FIRST NAME
B17-024	Smith	Fred
C12-392	Smith	Alice
A22-935	Smith	Henry
E44-523	Smith	Fred

Instead of a list of columns, we can say "*" to get all columns from the table. Thus:

```
select * from mytable
```

will output all columns from all records of the table, completely dumping the table.

We can sort the output with "order by" followed by a list of columns to sort by. The database engine first sorts by the first column specified. For all records with the same value for the first column, it sorts by the second column, etc.

Example:

```
select account_number, last_name, first_name
from customer
where last_name='Smith'
order by first_name, account_number
```

ACCOUNT NUMBER	LAST NAME	FIRST NAME
C12-392	Smith	Alice
B17-024	Smith	Fred
E44-523	Smith	Fred
A22-935	Smith	Henry

Note we have two customers named "Fred Smith", so the database engine sorts them by account_number.

There are several "aggregate functions" available to give information about sets of records.

"count(*)" givess the number of records meeting the condition.

"count(column)" gives the number of records with non-null values in the named column.

"sum(column)" gives the total of the values in the named column. Nulls are ignored. This is only legal for numeric columns, because it doesn't make sense to add dates or characters.

"min(column)" gives the smallest value occurring in the named column. For numbers this means the arithmetically smallest. For character it means the first alphabetically. For dates it means the earliest.

"max(column)" gives the largest value. It's the opposite of "min".

"avg(column)" gives the average value for the named column. Nulls are ignored. For example, the average of 2, 4, and null is 3. The null just doesn't count.

Example: Suppose this query ...

```
select account_number, account_type, balance
from account
order by account_number
```

gives

ACCOUNT_NUMBER	ACCOUNT_TYPE	BALANCE
0001	S	100
0002	S	300
0003	R	150
0004	R	350
0005	S	null

Then the query

```
select count(*), count(balance), sum(balance)
from account where account_type='S'
```

gives

COUNT(*)	COUNT(BALANCE)	SUM(BALANCE)
3	2	400

You can also get aggregate values for groups of records using the "group by" clause. You give a combination of fields on which to calculate the aggregate.

Example, using the same data as above:

```
select account_type, count(*), avg(balance)
from account
group by account_type
```

.gives

ACCOUNT_TYPE	COUNT(*)	AVG(BALANCE)
S	3	200
R	2	250

In standard SQL, any column not inside an aggregate must be included in the group-by. (Some database products give other options.)

An important feature of "select" is the ability to join two or more tables together. You can use a join instead of a simple table in a select. One format of join is:

```
table1 join table2 using (column1, ...)
```

The list of columns is columns to match that have the same name in both tables.

For example, suppose we have an student table with columns named student_id, first_name, and last_name. We also have a registration table with columns student_id, dept, class_num, and grade. Such as:

```
select * from student
```

STUDENT_ID	FIRST_NAME	LAST_NAME
0001	Robert	Anderson
0002	Mary	Babbit
0003	Jorge	O'Reilly
0004	Amy	Wong

```
select * from registration
```

STUDENT_ID	DEPT	CLASS_NUM	GRADE
0001	CS	101	A
0001	CS	102	B
0001	HI	204	B
0002	CS	102	C
0002	SC	302	D
0004	HI	204	B

We want to list all students registered in computer science (department 'CS') classes, with the student's name and grade. We have to join the two tables because neither table by itself has all the information we need.

```
select class_num, first_name, last_name, grade
from registration join student using
(student_id)
where dept='CS'
order by last_name, first_name
```

If more than one record from one of the tables matches a record on the other, the information from the "one" record is repeated. In this example, the output would be:

CLASS_NUM	FIRST_NAME	LAST_NAME	GRADE
101	Robert	Anderson	A
102	Robert	Anderson	B
102	Mary	Babbit	C

The plain "join" is what we call an "inner join". Data is only included in the output if a match is found on both tables. There are several kinds of "outer join". A "left outer join" -- or simply "left join" -- includes every record that occurs in the table on the left side of the word "join", even if there is no match against the right table. A "right outer join" -- or "right join" -- includes every record from the table on the right even if there is no match against the table on the left. A "full join" includes every record from either table regardless of matches. In any of these cases, any columns from the unmatched table show a value of null.

Example: Using the same tables above, list all the classes for each student. Include students with no classes.

```
select first_name, last_name, dept, class_num
from student left join registration using
(student_id)
```

FIRST_NAME	LAST_NAME	DEPT	CLASS_NUM
Robert	Anderson	CS	101
Robert	Anderson	CS	102
Robert	Anderson	HI	204
Mary	Babbit	CS	102
Mary	Babbit	SC	302
Jorge	O'Reilly		
Amy	Wong	HI	204

Note that Mr O'Reilly appears on the list with null department and class number because he is not registered for any classes.

When we join tables, we can specify which table a given column comes from with the "dot" notation: We write the table name, a dot, and the column name. For example, "student.student_id". If the same column name appears in more than one table, we must do this to distinguish them. We often do this even when the column names are unique to identify to the reader which table a column comes from.

A more general version of join is:

```
table1 join table2 on condition
```

"condition" can be any logical expression. When a matching column does not have the same name in both tables, we must use "on" rather than "using". Normally the condition involves comparisons of columns from the two tables. While "using" implies an "equals" test, with "on" you can use other sorts of tests, like less-than or like. You can also test fields in either table on their own, that is, not comparing them to a corresponding field in the other table.

Example: We want to know all the students who got a B in any class.

```
select first_name, last_name, dept, class_num
from student join registration
on student.student_id=registration.student_id
and registration.grade='B'
```

This gives

FIRST_NAME	LAST_NAME	DEPT	CLASS_NUM
Robert	Anderson	CS	102
Robert	Anderson	HI	204
Amy	Wong	HI	204

This gives exactly the same results as if we put the "registration.grade='B'" in a "where" clause. For an inner join, it doesn't matter whether "extra" conditions are put in the "on" clause or the "where" clause. The effect is the same. But for an outer join, it can matter. Conditions in an "on" clause are applied before joining the records, while conditions in the "where" clause are applied after joining the records. That is, in a left join, if an "on" condition excludes all records from the right-hand table, the record from the left-hand table can still be included, with nulls for the right table columns. The reverse is true for a right join. But a where clause would join first, then eliminate the record, so there might be no record at all.

Example: Let's take the above query and simply change the join to a left join.

```
select first_name, last_name, dept, class_num
from student left join registration
on student.student_id=registration.student_id
and registration.grade='B'
```

This gives

FIRST_NAME	LAST_NAME	DEPT	CLASS_NUM
Robert	Anderson	CS	102
Robert	Anderson	HI	204
Mary	Babbit	null	null
Jorge	O'Reilly	null	null
Amy	Wong	HI	204

But if we move the "grade" test to the "where" clause, that is:

```
select first_name, last_name, dept, class_num
from student left join registration
on student.student_id=registration.student_id
where registration.grade='B'
```

Then we get the same results as with the inner join.

A key feature of SQL "select" statements is that we tell the database what we want, not how to get it. In the above examples, we did not tell the database engine whether to first read the Student table and then look for matching Registration records, or to first look for Registration records and then find the matching Student record for each. Every SQL database engine has an "optimizer" that attempts to find the most efficient way to satisfy the query, or at least a fairly efficient way. A key factor in deciding how to optimize is the use of indexes. Speaking of which ...

5.6. Indexes

In a SQL database, indexes are purely a performance issue. There is no query or other function that will not work because an index is or is not present. The only difference is how fast it runs and how much disk space it takes.

An index allows a SQL query to find the desired records rapidly. But it takes time to update an index every time a record is added or changed, and the index consumes space on disk. So creating indexes is a trade-off. Indexes can give a huge speed-up to queries, but indexes which are rarely (or never) used cost more to maintain than they save on queries.

The general format to create an index is:

```
create index indexname on table (column,...)
```

For example:

```
create index ix_reg_1 on registration
(student_id, class_num)
```

(In some versions of SQL the index name is optional. The engine just invents a name. As you rarely refer to an index by name, this saves some trouble.)

The database engine can use an index to find records that meet a "where" condition more rapidly, or to retrieve records in the order called for by an "order by".

When an index is valuable is a more complex question than might at first appear.

The simplest case is when you search for a specific value or range of values, such as

```
select * from customer
where customer_number=12947
```

or

```
select * from customer_order
where order_date>='2008-01-01' and
order_date<='2008-12-31'
```

In this case an index on customer_number or order_date should always speed up the query.

It is also likely to help if we index any field used in a join. For example:

```
select *
from customer join customer_order using
(customer_number)
where customer.state='VA'
```

To satisfy this query, the database engine will probably first find all customers from Virginia, and then for each look up the corresponding orders using the customer_number. Therefore, indexes on both customer.state and customer_order.customer_number will likely improve the query.

But not necessarily. If the customer_order table is small and the customer table large, the database engine might decide to sequentially read the customer_order file and then look up the matching customer, so that an index on customer_order.customer_number would be useless. (We would expect there to be more customer_order's than customer's. Each customer should have at least one order. But perhaps we are including "prospective" customers, or perhaps we purge order data after a certain amount of time but keep the customer data so we can send them advertising.)

In addition to speeding up a "where", an index can be used to speed up an "order by". Suppose we have the query:

```
selet * from customer
order by customer_number
```

The optimizer can use an index on customer_number to read the records in the desired order, without having to sort them.

The database engine can't use two indexes on the same table for the same query: it must pick one or the other. So suppose you have a query like:

```
select * from customer
where state='VA' and discount>5
```

The database engine could use an index on state, or an index on discount. If you have indexes on both, it can only use one and will ignore the other. The engine will generally attempt to pick the one that will result in reading the fewest records.

When the optimizer has a choice between using an index to find the desired records, and using an index to get the records in the desired order, if usually chooses the "find" index and puts the records in order by sorting them in memory. If a table has 100,000 records of which we want 20, it makes a lot more sense to home in on just the 20 if possible and then sort them, then to read the 100,000 in order and have to skip over the 99,980 we don't care about. In practice this means that the results of most queries are sorted rather than using an index for ordering. On the other hand, suppose there are 100,000 records in the database of which we want 50,000. In that case it is likely more efficient to read 100,000 records and skip over half of them to avoid sorting such a large number of records.

You can create a single index that uses more than one column. This is the same concept as sorting on more than one column: the index behaves as if it first sorted all the records by the first column, and then for cases where the first column is the same, it sorts by the second column.

When you "order by" or join on all the columns in a multi-column index, the SQL engine can use the complete index. For example:

```
select * from employee join department on
employee.dept_id=department.dept_id and
employee.office_id=department.office_id
```

The SQL engine will read one of these tables sequentially and then look up the matching record or records in the other. An index on "(dept_id, office_id)" would likely be a big help.

The engine can also use just the leading columns in a multi-column index, if later columns are not mentioned or if they cannot be used for some other reason. Suppose we had:

```
select * from employee join department on
employee.dept_id=department.dept_id
```

Further suppose that it reads Employee sequentially and then looks up Department. An index on "department(dept_id)" would of course be useful. An index on "department(dept_id,office_id)" would be equally useful. The office_id would be ignored but SQL could take advantage of the dept_id. However, an index on "department(office_id,dept_id)" would be useless. As the engine doesn't know the office_id, it can't make much use of dept_id's within office_id's.

Less than and greater than tests can also take advantage of an index. The database engine can't jump directly to one record, but it can narrow down the range. Example:

```
select * from employee where dept_id>=200 and
dept_id<300
```

An index on dept_id would allow the database engine to skip directly to 200 and start reading from there. When it got to 300 it would know to stop.

Some database engines are smart enough to use an index for a "like" test if the first character is not wild. But if the first character is wild, there is no way an index is going to be useful. So

```
select * from product
where product_name like 'wood%'
```

could use an index on product_name, but

```
select * from product
where product_code like '_x-2'
```

would not benefit from an index on product_code.

You almost always want to create an index for each column containing a foreign key. If you ever want to find the child records from the parent, such an index will be useful. And one way or another, you always need a way to find child records when the parent is updated or deleted. Some database engines automatically create an index on any column declared to be a foreign key.

You can create an index on an expression rather than a stored column. Then the index can be used when a query tests the output of the function.

For example, suppose we want to search for customer names without regard to capitalization. Easy enough, we can write a query like:

```
select * from customer
where upper(customer_name)='SMITH'
```

But in this case, an index on customer_name is useless. "SMITH" is not equal to "Smith", so if the customer's name was entered with lower case it would not match. Indeed, recall that all lower case letters are less than all upper case letters. So an index on customer_name (with no "upper") would put "Sanders" after "SMITH" but before "Smith". If that's the only index we have, the database engine will be forced to sequentially read the entire customer table to find matching names.

But we can create this index:

```
create index ix_cust_u
on customer(upper(customer_name))
```

Now the above query can use this index and find the desired name very quickly.

(In my mySQL tests, this example did not apply, because mySQL does all tests case-insensitive, so all indexes on text columns are apparently the equivalent of upper(column). But the example works as described in Postgres. Other functions would apply equally well to mySQL.)

The optimizer considers what indexes are available when deciding how to execute your query. Consider the query:

```
select *
from customer_order join product using
(product_id)
where customer_order.order_type='B'
and product.in_stock=false
```

There are two obvious ways for the database engine to execute this query: It could read all the customer_order records, and then for each look up the matching product; or it could read all the product records, and then for each look up the matching customer_order.

If you have an index on order_type but not on in_stock, that will be a strong reason for the engine to decide to read customer_order first: It can then quickly select only the type "B" records and look up the matching product records from there. If it read product first it would have to read every product record, find the matching customer_order records, and then eliminate all those where the order type is not "B".

The full story is much more complicated than that, because available indexes are not the only factor. The optimizer also considers the relative sizes of the tables, and it keeps some statistics about the distribution of values. So in this example, if the optimizer knows that there are only three records in the entire product table that are not in stock, it might decide to read the product table first to home in on just those three records, regardless of the indexes.

5.7. Sequences

SQL provides a mechanism for assigning sequential numbers. That is, the first call will get "1", the second will get "2", etc. This is very handy when we want to identify records by a sequence number, and we want an absolute guarantee that the same number will never be assigned twice. (See section 9.2, Natural vs Synthetic Keys, and chapter 14, Implementation.)

To create a sequence, we use the command:

```
create sequence sequencename start start
increment inc
```

This creates a sequence that will start at "start" and add "inc" to it each time a new value is requested.

Example:

```
create sequence customerseq start 10
increment 3
```

This creates a sequence that first returns 10, then 13, then 16, etc.

"Start" and "inc" both default to 1, so if you write simply:

```
create sequence mycount
```

you get a sequence that counts 1, 2, 3, etc. This is usually want you want, so creating a "normal" sequence is pretty easy.

You retrieve values from a sequence with the "nextval(name)" function. You can also write "currval(name)" to get the same value last returned.

You could use this in a statement like this:

```
create sequence cust_seq
… some time later …
insert into customer (customer_id, name,
account_type)
values (nextval(cust_seq),'Hiram
Zelanski','BW')
```

The "nextval" assigns the next available number to the inserted record.

(None of the above worked in my mySQL tests because mySQL does not support sequences. mySQL has its own non-standard mechanism for assigning unique sequential numbers that involves declaring a column to be "auto_increment". These examples do work in Postgres.)

5.8.   Review Questions

1. What does "SQL" stand for and how do you pronounce it?

2. What are the major SQL data types? What kind of data can each contain?

3. What does "null" mean? What is it used for?

4. What is an "identifier" in SQL? What are the rules for an identifier?

5. What are the four types of expressions?

6. What are the arithmetic operators? What are the character operators? What are the logical operators?

7. What is the difference between DDL and DML?

8. What does the "create" statement do? What information do you normally include in a "create"?

9. What is a foreign key? What does SQL do to help you manage foreign keys?

10. What are the four basic DML commands? What does each one do?

11. What are the major parts of a "select" statement? What does each do?

12. How do indexes help us? How do we create an index?

13. How do sequences help us? How do we create a sequence?

6. ENTITIES

6.1. Definition

The first step in building a database is to figure out what entities it will contain.

An entity is a class of people, places, or things that exist in the real world, that is relevant to the current problem, about which we wish to keep information, and which has identifiable instances.

Let's look at this definition piece by piece.

An entity is a person, place, or thing. This should remind you of the elementary school definition of a noun. If you can't describe it with a noun or a short phrase that includes a noun, it is probably not an entity. "Product" could be an entity because "Product" is a noun.

"Build" is almost certainly not because "Build" is a verb. "Above" is almost certainly not because "Above" is a preposition. Etc.

Entities should be things that exist in the real world, outside of our computer system. "Disk drive", "Data entry clerk", and "Communication line" are not normally valid entities. Common entities in business systems are things like "Customer", "Manufactured Part", and "Office". (If you're creating a computer system to manage computer systems, this can get confusing, because things outside the computer system have the same names as things inside the computer system. But let's assume you have a more normal case.)

An entity must be relevant to the current system. Perhaps this sounds obvious, but inexperienced database designers often try to include all sorts of entities that may be part of the business but which have no reason to be part of the system that they are designing today. Suppose you are creating an order-processing system. "Customer" is a likely entity. "Employee" might or might not be an entity. If your system must keep track of which employee took a certain order, for example, it would be relevant. "Employee spouse" is almost certainly not an entity. Of course many of your employees are probably married. You might keep information about their spouses for an employee benefits system, as your company insurance likely covers spouses. But unless your company has a policy of holding an employee's wife for ransom until he meets his sales quota, it is unlikely that this would be a relevant entity in an order processing system.

There must be some information – some attributes – that we want to keep about an entity.

In a mail-order system, we surely need to know the state that a customer lives in so we can ship the merchandise to her. Is "state" an entity? That depends on whether we need to keep any information about the states. If, say, we have to track different tax information for different states, or if we estimate delivery time based on the state, then state would be an entity. But if all we do with state is record it as part of the customer's address, state is a data item we keep about the customer entity; it is not an entity itself.

Finally, an entity must have identifiable instances. An "instance" means an occurrence, one of something. For example, if we have an entity of Person, instances might be "Fred Smith" and "Mary Jones". We must be able to count how many of them there are, to name them or point at them, and there must be more than one. Person is a possible entity: There are many people in the world and they have names or other identifying information.

When I say that you should be able to point to the instances, this is usually literally true. Happiness is unlikely to be an entity because we can not say there is one happiness over here and another over there. Entity instances are normally physical, and if you're considering an example where they're not, you should examine it carefully. But it's not impossible. For example, a system for a synthetic food company might have an entity for Flavor – if they keep data about individual flavors.

The World is generally not an entity because there is only one that is of interest to us. If you are building a system to track astronomy information, then World might be an entity.

Some developers say that there are exceptions to the "more than one" rule. The most important is that there is often a valid reason to create an entity for "this system" with, of course, only one instance, in order to hold system-wide information, like preferred screen color or the date payroll was last run. I reply that that is not really an entity, even though we ultimately store it in the database in the same way that we store entities. It is a programming convenience that is outside of our true database design. Arguably this reply is hair-splitting and pedantic. Whatever.

6.2.   Consolidating Entities

When is a group of things one entity and when is it two or more entities?

Any customer account system likely has to handle many different types of transactions: sales, payments, refunds, etc. We could have one entity for Transaction that would include all of these things, or we could have separate Entities for each. Or in a human resources system, should we have separate entities for Employee and Retiree, or a single entity that includes both?

How do we decide? We have to consider what data we want to keep about each of these things and what processes we are likely to want to perform on them. If we have all the same data and use them all in the same way, then this is a single entity. If they have completely different data and completely different processes, then they are separate entities.

The hard question is when they are "mostly" or "partly" the same.

Some database designers say that if they have any different data at all, they are separate entities. By this standard, sales and payments cannot be instances of the same entity. They would share some attributes, like date and customer account and dollar amount. But they have some attributes that are different, like a payment would have payment method (cash, check, credit card), which would not apply to a sale; while a sale would have a product, which would not apply to a payment. If we try to put these in a single entity there will be attributes that are not applicable, and will have to be left blank or null or filled with dummy values. When we try to process them, we are going to have to interpret these blank or dummy values.

But this problem can be readily solved. One, we can simply live with it. Two, we can give a column a generic definition. Suppose we are considering whether to consolidate credit card payments and check payments in a single entity. For credit card payments we must store the credit card number. For check payments we must store the bank account number. We could create two attributes with the understanding that for any given record, one will be filled and the other left blank. Or we could create a single attribute and give it a somewhat generic name, like "account number", and let it store one or the other as appropriate. This is called "overloading".

That example is pretty tame, but this is a technique which can be abused. When we start saying that the field sometimes contains the co-signer name, sometimes the zip code, and sometimes the customer's birth date, things are getting silly. We'll discuss this issue further in chapter 8, Attributes.

The question of one or many is ultimately a practical one: Which way makes our lives easier?

When consolidating entities is a good idea, we should see two advantages:

One, making one entity instead of many means that our database design is simpler, and simple is good. The database is easier to understand and describe. We do not have to worry about synchronizing definitions across multiple entities. In the transaction example, if, say, we decide we need to increase the number of digits in the dollar amount attribute, we have to remember to increase it in all the relevant entities. In practice, keeping track of all the places it occurs and coordinating changes gets very difficult.

Two, having all the data in one entity simplifies our queries. In the transaction example, a very likely query is to find a customer's current balance. With a single entity, this is easy: find the total of the amount for all transactions. (If we can make the amounts signed – positive for credits and negative for debits or vice versa – then we can add them up with a single, simple query, like "select sum(amount) from transaction where customer=?".) If they're in multiple entities, we would have to write a more complex query to retrieve them all. As the questions we want to ask become more complicated, collecting information from multiple entities can become more and more difficult.

When combining entities is a bad idea, exactly the opposite happens.

One, the database design becomes convoluted. We find ourselves at a loss for what to call an entity because it includes very different ideas. A good sign that this is happening is when we are tempted to put conjunctions in the entity name, like "Customer or Employee". (When you start coming up with names like "Place or Product" you have almost surely run amok.) Any given record has many unused attributes, or our attributes are highly overloaded. The database design becomes difficult to explain.

Two, having unrelated data in one entity complicates our queries. Every query must check a "type code" to decide which records to include – or worse, we have to check many attributes using obscure rules which must be carefully written down somewhere (but never are). Before we can use an attribute's contents we must check if it contains relevant data. A sure sign of trouble here is if you find yourself checking if an attribute contains only digits before adding it to a total, etc.

Sometimes when we consolidate entities the unity is so complete that we think of this as a single entity and that is the end of the story. Other times we define an entity and "sub-entities", that is, the entity has multiple types, and these types behave differently under at least some circumstances.

Another option is to put common data in one entity and then create related entities to hold the data that is different, which are connected to the common entity. (See chapter 7, Relationships.) Some database designers prefer this because it is cleaner: it avoids having empty attributes and it avoids overloading. The drawback is that when we want the data for the sub-type, we have to find the related record in the other entity. This is a solution that looks great from an abstract, theoretical point of view, but is sometimes an annoying pain in practice. See section 7.2.3 for more on this.

(Note that this is the problem that Object-Oriented Databases set out to solve. See section 4.3.)

Adventures
in Real Life!

When a factory builds a product, they typically work with many different kinds of parts. They will start out with nuts and bolts and wires and pieces of sheet metal and sticks of plastic and wooden boards and so on. These are then assembled into higher-level components. For example, wire and metal and plastic may be combined to make an electric motor. Clearly, a motor is a very different thing from the pieces that make it up.

Nevertheless, people who develop Manufacturing Requirements Planning (MRP) systems – systems that help manage processes in a factory – have a slogan: "Parts is parts". Typically all the different kinds of parts that a factory might use get thrown into one entity: Parts. While they are made of many different materials and have many different characteristics, ultimately, from a factory's perspective, we want to do the same things to them: Buy them; store them somewhere until we're ready to use them; transform them in some way, like cutting, bending, and painting; assemble them into bigger and more complex parts; and sell them.

Some developers are tempted to separate raw materials from assemblies, or wood from metal. But such distinctions aren't relevant to a manufacturing system.

We may buy our motors from an outside supplier or we may build them ourselves, but either way, once the motor is built, we do the same things with it.

Etc. Parts is parts.

6.3.   Identifying Entities

A list of entities should be meaningful to the system users. It should include things that they are familiar with. But don't expect the user to be able to tell you what the entities are. Users often are confused about the database definition of an entity.

Still, a good place to start is by asking the user what people, places, and things are relevant to the system. Make a list. We will call these "candidate entities". Then scrub this list with reviews such as these. We start with the definition and go on to other criteria.

Any examples I give about scrubbing entities must be qualified with words like "usually" and "probably", because I cannot make definitive statements without knowing the details of the system you are trying to build and the terminology of your organization. Words that don't sound like entity names might be valid if they are being used in some technical or proprietary sense. For example, earlier I said that "Build" is not a valid entity name because it is a verb. But some organizations refer to a particular set of parts being assembled into a prototype as "a build". In this case they are using "build" as a noun, so it might well be a valid entity.

Evaluate every candidate entity against the definition. Is it a person, place, or thing? Does it exist outside the system? Does it have identifiable instances? Do we keep information about it?

Common issues that you will run into attempting to scrub a user-prepared list of candidate entities include:

One: Users who know a little bit about computer systems often have a problem with the "outside the system" rule. "A little knowledge is a dangerous thing." Users often mix the real requirements for what the system must accomplish – process orders or schedule flights or whatever – with preconceived ideas about how to do this on the computer.

Two: Users sometimes include abstract ideas as candidate entities, like "Quality" or "Customer Service". These things might possibly be entities, if we are actually talking about a quality rating of some kind or complaints to the customer service department. More often they're just general ideas. This is a violation of the identifiable instances rule. Can you point out an example of "quality" to me? Not a product that has high quality – that would be an instance of "Product" – but can you point to a block of quality itself?

Three: In common language we often have many different words for the same thing. Sometimes what is really the same entity will show up multiple times on candidate entity lists. For example, if we have both "Customers" and "Clients", these are probably the same thing. The caveat about "usually" applies here: We must be sure that we understand the definitions. Two terms that are synonyms in everyday speech may have specialized meanings in the context of our system and really be quite different. Perhaps "Customers" refers to people who shop at our store while "Clients" are advertisers. Likewise, two things that sound different may really be the same.

Four: Users often confuse an entity instance with an entity. They will say that we must have an entity for the West Region and an entity for the East Region. Most likely, these are not entities themselves but instances of the Region entity. This is less obvious when the names are more subtle. If I had used as the example Domestic and Foreign, you might have been fooled. One sign here is when they use an adjective as an entity name. The adjective must modify some noun. If you realize that two adjectives must modify the same noun, it is likely that you have found the real entity. (Another possibility here is that the candidate entity is really a sub-entity within some larger entity.)

6.4.   Review Questions

1.   What is an entity? What part of speech corresponds to an entity?

2.   What are the five parts of the definition of an entity?

3.   When should we make a group of things a single entity and when should we make it multiple entities?

4.   What is "attribute overloading"?

7. RELATIONSHIPS

Assumptions are the termites of relationships.

-- Henry Winkler

7.1. Definition

A relationship is a connection or association between two entities. A relationship is named with a verb or verb phrase. We write the relationship as first-entity relationship second-entity.

For example, suppose we have the entities "Employee" and "Department". We might then have the relationship "Employee works-for Department".

Perhaps the most common kind of relationship is this kind of membership in a group. Voter lives-in Precinct, Book is-about Subject, etc.

A relationship can also be a verb in the more "active" sense. Factory makes Product, Supervisor approves Paycheck, etc.

We can name the relationship so that the entities appear in either order. For example, we can say Truck delivers Package or we can say Package is-delivered-by Truck. It makes no difference. Pick the one that reads most naturally or is more convenient for whatever reason.

An entity can have a relationship with itself. A classic example of this is a company organization chart, where there is a president at the top, vice-presidents beneath him, perhaps regional managers beneath them, then branch managers, then supervisors, and finally down to the peasant workers. Each employee has a supervisor, so we have the relationship Employee reports-to Employee. This doesn't mean that an employee reports to himself, but rather than the person he reports to is another employee, who in turn may well report to yet another employee, etc. A relationship that connects an entity to itself is called a "recursive relationship".

Note that in the org chart example, the president of the company – or CEO or whatever the title of the top dog is -- doesn't report to anyone. This is perfectly acceptable and normal. It may or may not be required for every instance of an entity to participate in any given relationship. In a Part is-made-from Part relationship, any Part that is an end item – something we sell to our customers – will not have a parent. There could be many of these.

7.2. Characteristics

Every relationship has two important characteristics: cardinality and obligation.

7.2.1. Cardinality

Cardinality means how many instances of each entity are involved in the relationship. We usually just worry about "one" or "many", where "many" is any number more than one. This is not a radical concept: it's the same idea as "singular" versus "plural". The cardinality of a relationship is expressed as the cardinality of each end. Thus, a relationship can be "one-to-one", "one-to-many", or "many-to-many". These can be abbreviated "1:1", "1:M", or "M:M". Of course in a 1:M relationship, we have to make clear which end is the "one" and which is the "many".

Examples:

An order has many line items. We have an "Order" entity and a "Line Item" entity, and then we have an "Order has Line Item" relationship that is 1:M, one order to many line items.

Students attend classes. A student attends many different classes, and each class has many students. Therefore the relationship is M:M.

Some employees have an individual retirement plan. The relationship between Employee and Retirement-Plan is 1:1. (By "individual retirement plan" I mean that the entity instance is for that one employee, not the company plan in general.)

Occasionally it is useful to talk about a number other than one or many. Sometimes a relationship is logically limited to exactly three or whatever number. For example, the relationship of U.S. State to Senator is exactly one-to-two. We can never have three senators from a single state. But these occasions are rare. We normally simply call them one-to-many and note the logical limit somewhere.

7.2.2. Obligation

Obligation means that the entity at either end of the relationship may be required to participate in that relationship in order to exist. We say that each end is "obligatory" or "non-obligatory". If it is obligatory, then an instance of that entity must have the relationship.

Examples:

Some employees have an individual retirement plan. An employee is not required to have a retirement plan, so the relationship is non-obligatory on the employee side. An individual retirement plan cannot exist without an employee, so it is obligatory on the retirement plan side.

An order has many line items. A line item cannot exist without being part of some order. The relationship is obligatory on the line item side.

This brings us to a difficult but common case. Can an order exist without having any line items? On the one hand, an order that isn't an order for anything sounds pretty meaningless. On the other hand, we run into a timing issue. If an order can't exist without line items but line items can't exist without an order, which do we create first? It's a chicken-and-egg problem. This may be solved if our system is capable of adding both simultaneously, though that can be tricky. What happens if a customer orders an item, then changes his mind, cancels it, and orders a different item? In between deleting the old item and adding the new one, the order has no items.

We might also have to make a seemingly obligatory relationship non-obligatory if there is the possibility that although the relationship must exist in the real world, we may not have the information immediately. Example: We have a genealogy system with the relationship Person child-of Person. Clearly this is non-obligatory on the "parent" side: not everyone has children. Logically, it is obligatory on the "child" side: everyone must have parents. Except ... yes, everyone has parents, but maybe at the time we enter someone into the system we don't know who their parents are. The whole point of a genealogy system is surely that we want to build up data as we discover the relationships. We don't want to insist that you know it all before you start. Furthermore, the chain has to start *somewhere*. If we go all the way back to Adam, he doesn't have any parents. We're going to start somewhere, and wherever we start, we won't have parents for that person.

Thus, even if we think of a relationship as obligatory, it is really non-obligatory if there can ever legitimately be a period of time -- however brief, even a fraction of a second --when the relationship does not exist. Usually this happens for timing reasons: We just haven't had a chance to enter the other end of the relationship yet because we have to do something first, or we can't enter the relationship yet because we don't have all the information.

7.2.3. Why One-to-One?

Some designers wonder why we would ever create a one-to-one relationship. It two entities always go together, aren't they the same entity? If we are tempted to create an entity to hold employee hire information and another to hold employee benefits information, wouldn't it make more sense to just roll these together as Employee?

At the logical model level, we should keep them separate if they represent distinctly different ideas. Sometimes the relationships are not clear if attached to a single entity that combines both ideas.

One common example of this is sub-types and super-types, like we discussed in section 6.2. We may create a 1:1 relationship between an entity that contains the common data for multiple sub-types, and each of the entities for the various sub-types. For example, we might have a Transaction entity with two sub-types, Charge and Payment.

There is then a 1:1 relationship between Charge and Transaction and another between Payment and Transaction.

When should we combine them and when should we keep them separate?

Suppose we are building a vote counting system. Obvious entities are Candidate and Voter. But every Candidate is also a Voter – surely he makes every effort to vote for himself – and the relationship is clearly 1:1, so someone might suggest that we combine Candidate and Voter into a single entity.

This is probably a bad idea. We now have relationships like "Voter votes-for Voter", which is very confusing just to read about, never mind trying to write the programs for this in a sensible way. Getting a list of candidates now requires figuring out which Voters are candidates. These are not the same entity.

A much better case could be made for combining Employee Hire and Employee Benefits. Even if an employee does not participate in the benefits program, we can probably just leave attributes blank or have some place to mark "no".

When making this decision, consider the obligation. If the relationship is obligatory on both ends, there's a much stronger case for combining them then if it is not.

In the logical model, we do not and should not consider efficiency and performance issues. No matter what you may now about database performance characteristics, save it for the Physical Model, chapter 12. Right now we're only concerned about the logical view.

"IF YOU WANT A RELATIONSHIP WITH ME, DB, IT HAD BETTER BE ONE-TO-ONE."

7.3. Defining Relationships

Some Entities only make sense in association with another entity. When a record cannot be understood except as it relates to a record in another entity, we call this a "defining relationship". Relationships that do not meet this are called "non-defining relationships".

Example: There is a 1:M relationship between Order and Line Item. It is meaningless to talk about a Line Item that is not part of some Order. It is difficult to imagine a Line Item moving from one Order to another. The most obvious key for Line Item is Order Number plus Line Number. This is a defining relationship.

There is also a 1:M relationship between Ship and Sailor. But it is not at all difficult to imagine a Sailor who is not presently assigned to any Ship. Perhaps he is a new recruit who has not yet been assigned to a ship, or he is presently assigned to shore duty. It is easy to imagine a sailor being transferred from one ship to another. It is unlikely that we would identify a sailor by what ship he was assigned to. That is, whatever identifying code or number we use for a sailor, we probably wouldn't call him "USS Constitution #327". This is not a defining relationship.

There is a connection between obligation and defining, but they are not the same. A defining relationship must be obligatory, but not every obligatory relationship is defining.

7.4. Entity-Relationship Diagrams

7.4.1. Basics

A very useful tool for helping us to decide what entities and relationships we need and to communicate them to others is the Entity-Relationship Diagram, or ERD.

On an ERD, we represent entities with rectangles and relationships with lines connecting the rectangles. In the entity box we write the name of the entity. If a relationship has a name, we write it along the line.

See the example in Figure 7.1.

Some experts draw a diamond in the middle of the line and write the relationship name inside the diamond, like in Figure 7.2. Personally I don't do this because it makes the diagram busier without adding any information. If

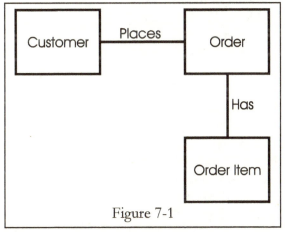

Figure 7-1

many (or all) of your relationships have names and you have a complex diagram with many crossed lines, it might be useful to include the diamonds to avoid confusion about which name goes with which line.

7.4.2. Cardinality and Obligation

We also want to identify the cardinality and obligation of relationships. There are several different schemes for doing that. Four common schemes are shown in Figure 7.3.

The Crow's Foot notation is probably the most popular, but in this book I'll use the Double-Arrow notation for the simple reason that I like it best.

I don't like the Arrow notation because it makes no distinction between "one" and "don't know". When we're drawing ERDs we often find that we don't know all the answers yet. A notation which does not give us any way to clearly identify "don't know" is lacking. (Or for that matter, "I forgot to fill it in.")

I have a similar objection to Crow's Foot. The symbol for "one" and the symbol for "obligatory" are the same: a cross-bar. If we draw both the obligation and the cardinality, this is no problem. If there are two cross-bars, this must mean "one" and "obligatory". If there is one cross-bar and one crow's foot, this must mean "many" and "obligatory". And if there is one empty circle and one cross-bar, this must mean "one" and "non-obligatory". But what if we haven't figured out one of these things yet? If we see just a cross-bar, there is no way to tell whether the writer meant that it is

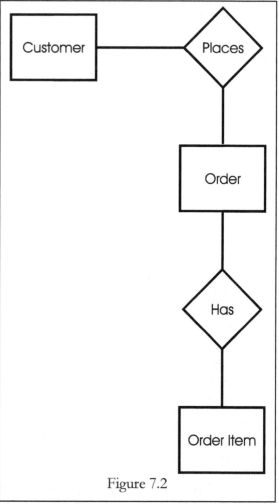

Figure 7.2

"one" and he didn't know the obligation, or that it is obligatory and he didn't know the cardinality.

The Algebraic notation has no accepted way to represent obligation. Some write "0-1" or "0-M" for non-obligatory and "1-1" or "1-M" for obligatory. Besides, this method is just esthetically un-appealing.

Thus, I prefer Double-Arrow as the most clear and unambiguous. I also find the idea of one arrowhead for "one" and two arrowheads for "more than one" very intuitive. And it's easy to draw.

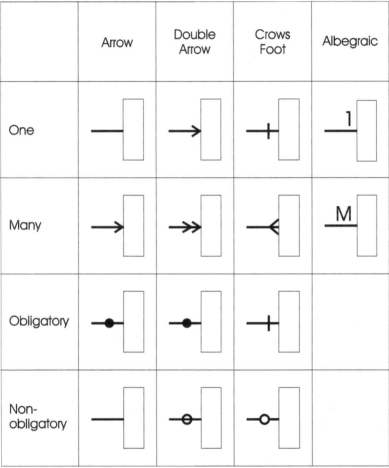

Figure 7.3

So a more complete ERD would look like Figure 7.4. In this example, the relationship between Customer and Order is 1:M (one-to-many), non-obligatory on the Customer side and obligatory on the Order side. That is, a Customer can have many Orders, but each Order is for just one Customer. A Customer can exist without having any Orders, but an Order cannot exist without having a Customer. The relationship between Order and Order Item is also 1:M, non-obligatory on the Order side and obligatory on the Order item side.

Be sure to put the obligation and cardinality symbols on the correct end of the line. In the above example, Customer-Order is one-to-many, i.e. one Customer for many Orders. So we put the "one" symbol on Customer and the "many" symbol on Order. That seems

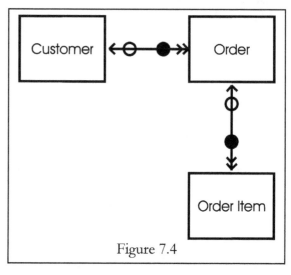

Figure 7.4

straightforward enough. Some people have trouble with which end to put the obligation symbol on. Customer-Order is obligatory for Order and non-obligatory for Customer. That is, we can have a Customer with no Orders, but we cannot have an Order with no Customer. So the "obligatory" symbol goes on Order: An Order must participate in the relationship to exist. A "non-obligatory" symbol goes on Customer. A Customer does not have to participate in the relationship to exist.

7.4.3. Special Cases

Some analysts use a solid line for defining relationships and a dotted line for non-defining relationships. I will not use that notation in this book, nor mark defining relationships any other way. I have never worked on a project where discussing this was useful: It's usually obvious and uninteresting which relationships are defining to all involved so we don't need to talk about. If you are working on a project where there is confusion or disagreement about defining relationships, than you certainly should identify them.

We show a recursive relationship – a relationship between an entity and itself – by bending the relationship line back around to the same entity. Any other relationships attach normally. See Figure 7.5.

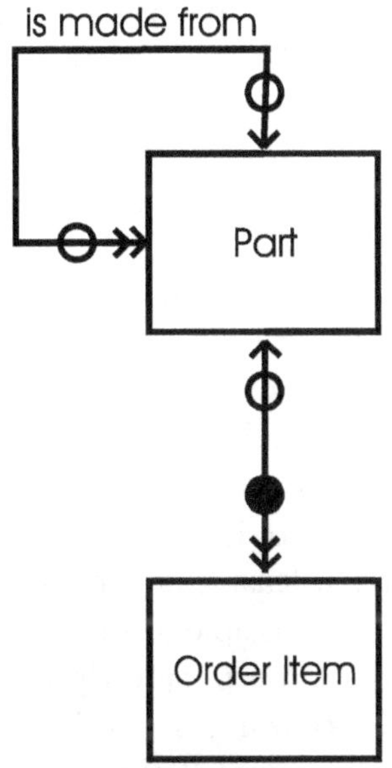

You may recall that in section 6.2 we discussed entities that have sub-types. Sometimes we consolidate all the sub-types into a single entity. There may be relationships that apply only to some sub-types and not others.

I show this on an ERD by drawing separate boxes for the sub-types, and then connecting these to the super-type with dotted lines. (As opposed to the solid lines used for relationships.) I draw relationships that apply to all sub-types with the connection going to the super-type, and relationships that apply only to a sub-type with the connection going to the appropriate

is made from

Part

Order Item

Figure 7.5

sub-type. See Figure 7.6. In this example, a magazine publisher accepts two types of orders: subscriptions, which of course are orders for all new issues as they are published; and back orders, which are orders for a specific issue. Every order must have a customer, but subscriptions connect to a magazine in general while back orders connect to a specific issue.

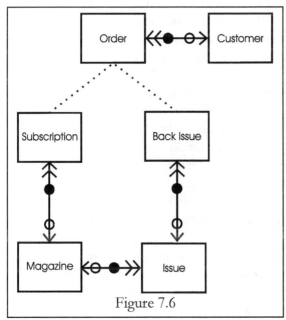

Figure 7.6

Note that it is not possible to directly implement sub-types on most relational database products, so this distinction will be lost when we create the physical model. But it can be very useful during the logical model stage when we are analyzing the organization of the data.

7.4.4. Mechanics

We typically build an ERD a little at a time as we figure things out. Start out by drawing the most obvious entities. Then try to discover or figure out the relationships between them. As you discover more entities, add them to the ERD.

Of course a real ERD has a whole lot more than three entities. These are just textbook examples. Most ERDs I have worked on have had at least a dozen or so entities. Some systems have hundreds. It is rarely possible to fit a readable ERD on a sheet of letter-sized paper.

Some people draw ERDs with paper and pencil. But this is the 21st century, so today we have software tools to help. Computer Associates ERWin is specifically designed to draw ERDs. Microsoft Visio has ERDs among the diagram types it supports. Any drawing tool should be useable. I drew the example diagrams in this book using CorelDraw. I actually prefer that over some of the custom ERD programs because it is more flexible. It does have the drawback that as it is not designed to draw ERDs, it often takes extra steps.

A practical problem when drawing ERDs is trying to arrange the entities so that the relationship lines don't cross. Programs designed to draw ERDs include tools to help rearrange the entities and untangle the lines. Any vector drawing program will let you move the entities around manually.

Some people draw little semi-circle "bridges" where two relationship lines cross. This is a notation borrowed from electrical diagrams, where we have to make clear whether two wires are connected or if we just had to draw the lines crossing because the diagram is cluttered. This is superfluous in ERDs. There is no need to distinguish two lines that connect from two lines that just happened to cross over each other, because there is no such thing as two relationships connecting. It's always an incidental product of drawing the picture. Of course, many crossing lines can make an ERD difficult to read. If we allow multi-entity relationships, as described in the next section, there is more possible ambiguity.

7.5.   Multi-Entity Relationships

Some experts say that a relationship must always connect exactly two entities. (Counting a recursive relationship as connecting two entities that happen to both be the same entity.) Others allow a relationship to connect three or more.

If you find the database design easier to understand with a multi-entity relationship, I'm not going to tell you that you can't do it. But such relationships are usually unnecessarily complex.

In most cases you can avoid a multi-entity relationship by rethinking the connections. Suppose you are tempted to define a relationship connecting Salesman, Customer, and Order. This might sound plausible at first: the three clearly go together in an intuitive sense. But the database design will be simpler if we break this into two relationships: one connecting Order and Salesman, another connecting Order and Customer. See Figure 7.7. Clearly every order has some customer, and presumably every order was made by some salesman. (Perhaps allowing for special cases like self-checkout.) Two relationships express the idea neatly. The only real connection between Salesman and Customer is through the sale, so we don't need to complicate the discussion with a three-way.

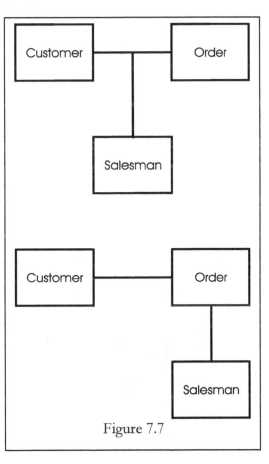

Figure 7.7

Sometimes breaking up the relationship like this doesn't make sense. But you can always achieve the same effect as a multi-entity relationship by defining an entity to serve as a "junction" and connecting all the original entities to this junction. Suppose you are tempted to define a relationship connecting Student, Tutor, and Subject. Unlike the order example, you can't just break this into two relationships. The relationship between Student and Tutor is not complete without stating the Subject. The relationship between Tutor and Subject is not complete without identifying the Student. Etc. But what you can do is create a "junction" entity. Create a "Tutor Assignment" entity that serves as a connection point for Students, Tutors, and Subjects. See Figure 7.8.

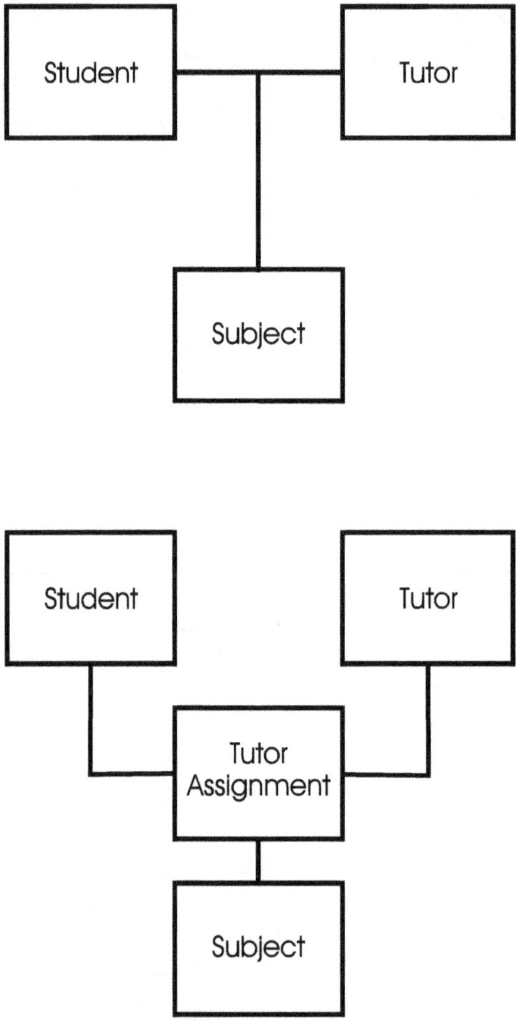

Cardinality is a problem in multi-entity relationships. If in the "tutor" example above we said that Tutor is "many", does that mean that a Student can have many Tutors, that a Subject can have many Tutors, or both? Breaking out the junction entity resolves this ambiguity.

Figure 7.8

- 78 -

(When we get to the Physical Model in chapter 12, we are effectively going to do this anyway. The only question is how we describe it in the logical model.)

7.6. Review Questions

1. What is a relationship?

2. What is "cardinality"?

3. What is "obligation"?

4. What is an Entity Relationship Diagram? What symbols are used on an ERD for (a) entities, (b) relationships, (c) cardinality, and (d) obligation?

5. What is a multi-entity relationship? Describe two ways to eliminate a multi-entity relationship.

8. ATTRIBUTES

Thing, body, matter, are nothing apart from the combinations of the elements - the colors, sounds, and so forth - nothing apart from their so-called attributes.

-- Ernst Mach

8.1. Definition

Attributes are any information we want to record about an entity.

An attribute must have distinct, identifiable values; hold a single fact; and have only one home in the database.

Attributes can be of a variety of data types. We typically list four possible data types:

Text: Such as a name or description.
Number: Such as count, measurement, monetary value.

Date: A point in time.

Boolean or Logical: True/false or yes/no.

This is not intended to be an exhaustive list, though in practice almost any information can be represented with one of these. For example, suppose we want our attribute to have a type of "color". Color isn't one of the listed types, but we could surely represent colors with the text of a color name, e.g. "red" or "turquoise"; or by a numeric representation, like a measure of the amount of each primary color.

8.2. Identifiable Values

When I say that attributes must have "identifiable values", I don't mean that you have to be able to list all possible values. "Distance" is a perfectly valid attribute, though listing every possible distance would be a formidable task. I mean that you must be able to attach a value to something for it to be an attribute. When I say "distinct values", I mean that different instances of the entity must have different values. Not that no two can be alike, but that they cannot all be the same.

For example, if we have an entity of "Product", likely attributes include "Description", "Cost", and "Date Sold". You can easily imagine distinct, identifiable values for such attributes. A description of one product might be "Toaster" while another would be "Microwave oven". One might have a price of $9.95 and another has a price of $59. Etc.

Most attributes ultimately end up as a blank on a screen or a form, or as a column on a report A good rule of thumb is that if it would not make sense to display the attribute name next to a blank for someone to fill in a value, or to print the attribute name as a column heading on a report with values beneath it, then this is probably not a valid attribute.

Consider the ever-popular order entry system example. When the customer places an order, we likely want to have blanks on a screen labeled "Name", "Address", and "Credit card number". People would have no problem associating a value with these and filling them in. But what if we were considering an attribute of, say, "Shipping department" or "Monday"? What value would a user enter beside one of these labels? If in your system you can really give a rational answer to this question, if you say that the value of Monday is true or false indicating whether the customer's home planet has meteor showers on Mondays or some such, then this could be a valid attribute. (Though simply calling it "Monday" is a poor choice of names in such a case.) If your only answer is, "Well, umm, Monday is a day of the week", but you can't attach some value to it for your system, then it's not an attribute.

Adventures in Real Life!

I briefly helped on a system for a bicycle marathon. One user included on his list of candidate attributes, "air pump". But as another team member asked, "What is the value of 'air pump'?" The user replied, "To inflate the tires". True, but not what we mean by "value" in this context. "Air pump" is probably not a valid attribute because there is no text or number or date that we would attach to it for a given instance. We would not say that this bicycle has an air pump of 7 while another bicycle has an air pump of 12.

(Again, the "probably" caveat. If different bicycles have different sizes or kinds of air pumps and this is something we care about in our system, "air pump" might be a valid attribute. In this case, one bicycle might have an air pump of "Acme model 324" while another has "Peerless style C".)

If you cannot attach a value of some type to a candidate attribute, then it isn't a real attribute.

8.3.   Single Fact

When I say an attribute must hold a single fact, I mean that there must be one fact per attribute and one attribute per fact. The catch phrase is "one fact per field".

Many systems combine unrelated information into a single attribute. There are three common ways that this happens.

8.3.1. Concatenated Attributes

The most obvious is the concatenated attribute, where two attributes are simply rammed together. These are often easy to

---

recognize: the description includes the words "and", "followed by", or similar terms, and the values have hyphens or slashes or other separator characters. When we find ourselves saying, "This attribute is the store number followed by a hyphen and the customer number", our own words should warn us that this is a concatenated attribute.

It is only a concatenated attribute if it is two separate facts *within the context of our system*. Social Security numbers are made up of three pieces each of which has meaning to the Social Security administration. To them, this is three separate attributes. But for most systems, we don't carry about the "internal structure" of a Social Security Number -- it's all just one big blob to us.

The easy test is: Will this system ever have to break the attribute into pieces? If the answer is yes, then break it apart once and keep it that way. The reality of computer systems is that it is easier to put two things together than to take them apart. If I have a jar of water and a jar of alcohol, I can easily mix them in any desired ratio. But try taking a jar where they've already been mixed and separate them out!

8.3.2. Character-by-Character

Another common mistake is to build a code where each letter means something. People seem to delight in creating codes that attempt to imbed all sorts of information into one character string.

 Adventures in Real Life!

Every car made in North America and Europe has a Vehicle Identification Number. This is built using a complex scheme.

Character 1: Country in which the vehicle was built. 1 or 4 = US, 2 = Canada, 3 = Mexico, J = Japan, K = Korea, S = England, W = Germany, Z = Italy. Etc.

Character 2: Manufacturer. G = General Motors, F = Ford, C = Chrysler, H = Honda, D = Mercedes Benz, V = VW, etc

Character 3: Division within a company. For example, within General Motors, 1 is Chevrolet passenger cars and C is Chevy trucks.

Characters 4-8: Varies by manufacturer. Used to identify body style, engine size, etc.

Character 9: Check digit.

Character 10: Model year. A = 1980, B = 1981, C = 1982, etc. Each year is assigned the next sequential letter of the alphabet, excluding I, O, Q, U, and Z. Then they start in on digits, excluding zero. That ends up with 9 = 2009, so 2010 starts over with A.

Character 11: Assembly plant where vehicle was made.

Characters 12-17: Serial number. Manufacturers may include other codes in here. For small manufacturers (less than 500 cars per year), positions 12 – 14 are combined with positions 1 – 3 to make up an "extended manufacturer identifier".

The above is how it works in North America. Europe has a slightly different scheme.

The VIN is at least seven different attributes crammed into one "super attribute", more in some cases. Any application attempting to work with this will have to constantly take it apart and put it back together. Any attempt to build indexes on this will have to index on the middle of a field. (Most database products can do this, but it's awkward.)

People who invent such codes apparently find it necessary to cram each real attribute into just one character, so we end up with obscure values like "S" for England and "C" for 1982. Then they run out of values so they have to recycle the codes, so "C" is also 2012.

Perhaps someone will argue that the VIN is useful because it is stamped on the car in several places, so someone can read a VIN off a car and immediately know all sorts of things about the vehicle.

But so what? There's surely a brand name badge on the vehicle anyway, so no one's going to look at the VIN to tell if this is a Ford or a Chevy. It's hard to see who would care what factory a car was built in and that sort of thing, and if customs officials or accident investigators or whomever need to know, they could surely access a database. If any information was really believed to be of value to the average potential buyer or mechanic, wouldn't it make more sense to print it somewhere in plain form where people could understand it without having to look up all the strange codes?

Let's concede one point to the inventors of the VIN: There is a valid reason to embed a manufacturer id in a sequence number. The goal is to have a unique identifier for every vehicle made anywhere in the world. If we tried to do this with a simple sequence number, then all the manufacturers in the world would have to be connected to a common computer system and constantly be asking for the next available number, with proper controls in place to insure that no two manufacturers were ever given the same number. If any manufacturer, anywhere in the world, had a problem with their connection to this database, the whole scheme would fall apart. A common solution to such a problem is to give each company a code that is used as the first few digits or characters of the identifier, and then they assign values within that. That way each company has its own set or pool of numbers to allocate. I don't consider this a violation of "one fact per field". You're free to insist that it is by a technical definition, but it is so useful that it's forgivable. (See chapter 16, Flexing the Model, for more discussion of when it's good to break the rules.)

8.3.3. Status Codes

Finally, there is the "status code". Often in our system we have a variety of conditions that might be true of a record at any given time. For example, an order might be "routine" or "priority". It also might be "unshipped" or "shipped". As I've stated it, these are clearly two unrelated things and should be two attributes. But we often see such things crammed into a single attribute, with values for all the possible combinations.

Adventures in Real Life!

I worked on a system that managed military technical manuals. The old system I inherited had an attribute they called "symbol code", which was a one-character attribute that includes values such as:

E "sponsor approval" (must get special authorization to obtain a copy)

T "time compliance" (manual describes a one-time job that must be completed by a specified date, like installing new equipment)

A ammunition-related
P preliminary (early draft of a new book)
C classified
Etc, for many other values.

This is a one position code with all these un-related possible values. What if we had a preliminary edition of an ammunition-related book for a time compliance task that required sponsor approval? There's only room to say one of these things. How do we pick which one?

Our team broke this attribute into separate attributes for each idea: A true/false for sponsor approval, another true/false for time compliance, a code for various levels of security classification, etc.

Adventures
in Real Life!

Sometimes developers try to solve the problem of multiple unrelated values by making codes for all possible combinations.

A military procurement system had a code for "business type" with the following values:

1	small business owned by a woman
2	small business owned by an economically disadvantaged person
3	small business owned by other
4	medium business owned by a woman
5	medium business owned by an economically disadvantaged person
6	medium business owned by other
7	large business owned by a woman
8	large business owned by an economically disadvantaged person
9	large business owned by other

These are three completely different attributes crammed into one -- business size, owner gender, and owner economic status. The developer tried to invent codes for every possible combination: Note the interesting combination of owning a large business *and* being economically disadvantaged.

There are several problems with combining multiple facts into a single attribute.

One: The queries become complex and obscure. For example, suppose in the "business type" example we want a list of all medium business owned by a woman. In that case we must admit that the combined field would be simpler. The query would simply say "where business_type='4'". With separate fields we would have to write "where business_size='M' and owner_gender='F'".

But suppose we want to find all woman-owned business. With the combined field, we would have to write "where business_type='1' or business_type='4' or business_type='7'". With separate fields it would simply be "where owner_gender='F'".

Even combinations that match the code can be obscure. Which is more clear: "where business_type=1 or business_type=4", or "where owner_gender='F' and (business_size='S' or business_size='M')"? Queries with separate fields are not only more flexible, they are also more "natural" and readable.

Two: Developers often fail to provide for all the possible combinations. The symbol code example, where the developer apparently didn't think of any possible combinations, is extreme. But often developers only allow for the obvious ones or the ones that have happened already. Even when someone makes a serious effort to include all the combinations, as they apparently did with the "business type" example, it's easy to miss some. What if the owner is both a woman and economically disadvantaged? There's no way to say that. Perhaps for their immediate purpose one or the other took priority, but then we are building into our database that this priority can never change.

The number of possibilities can easily get out of hand. In the symbol code example, even if we only include the five things listed above and even if they each had just two possibilities, that still makes $2^5 = 32$ combinations. This can be particularly easy to mess up when new values are added.

Note that I am not saying here that status codes are bad. They are perfectly good and valid. I am saying that each status should get its own attribute.

8.4.   One Home

When I say that every attribute must have one home in the database, I mean that each attribute must belong to only one entity. Developers sometimes repeat the same data in multiple entities.

There are (at least) three types of redundancy, which I'll call "vertical", "horizontal", and "aggregate".

8.4.1.   Vertical Redundancy

In vertical redundancy, the same data is repeated in multiple instances of the same entity. Usually this happens because data was put in the wrong entity. Entity instances that should be sharing a value instead each have their own. For example, suppose we have a database with information about our employees. We might have a "Department" entity and an "Employee" entity. Where does "Department Manager" belong? Surely this belongs in the Department entity. If we put it in Employee, we're going to have to repeat the Department Manager for every Employee. (If two employees in the same department can really have different department managers, then this person isn't really the "department manager", but something else.)

That example might seem obvious, but I've seen many like it in real life. Usually this comes from users who don't grasp the concept of an entity, though I'm sure developers often do this to themselves, too. You might think that when the user says he keeps a certain piece of information, he would know what that information is *about*. But they don't. I once had a user put "Store Phone Number" as an attribute of Sale. Barring the unlikely possibility that we set up a separate phone line for each customer, it's more likely that Store Phone Number is an attribute of Store. But, the user objected, the phone number goes on the sales receipt, so it must be an attribute of the sale! The reply is that a Sale is related to a Store, so if we want to know the Store Phone Number for a given Sale, we get it via the Store.

In that example it was easy to spot the user's mistake, but in other cases you have to really understand how the organization operates to know the right answer. I've had many discussions with users where I've had to very carefully ask, "What 'level' is this associated with?" Like, "Is the product price the same in all your stores, or does each store set its own price, or is there a more complex rule?"

We'll discuss vertical redundancy further in chapter 13, Normalization.

8.4.2. Horizontal Redundancy

Horizontal redundancy is when the same attribute is included in multiple related entities.

Adventures
in Real Life!

I worked on a system for a chain of retail stores. They had an entity for "Stock" that included information about each item that passed through the company's hands, like the supplier they bought it from, a part number, several fields for style and options, the cost, the date they sold it, etc. They also had an entity for "Sale", that included information about each item sold, including the supplier they bought it from, a part number, several fields for style and options, the cost, the date it was sold, etc. That is, almost all the information in the Sale entity was duplicated in the Stock entity. Updates routinely updated both places.

I suspect this was done because they also had Sale records for services, like delivery and repairs, for which there was no corresponding stock record – they didn't keep a warehouse full of "delivery" or "repair". So they had to keep all this information somewhere for services, and decided to put it in Sale. But they couldn't just put all the information about stocked items in Sale, because they had to record information about items in the warehouse before they were sold. That is, an unsold item would have a stock but no sale; a service would have a sale but no stock.

The right answer would be to create an additional entity with information about the item or service, distinct from whether it was stocked in the warehouse and equally distinct from whether it was sold.

What's wrong with this?

Perhaps the most obvious problem is that storing the same information multiple times is a waste of space. Maybe that's not such a big problem in these days of cheap disks. But no matter how cheap your disk drives are, if you waste enough space, sooner or later it's going to cost you.

The bigger problem is maintaining consistency. If you store the same information twice, then any time you update one place, you have to be sure to make the same update to the other. And if your programs do not guarantee 100% that this happens every time, then you can have inconsistent data. How do we interpret this? Suppose in our banking system at some point we misplace a decimal point, so the account status screen says that a customer has a balance of $20 and the account history screen shows his final balance as $2000. Which is it? What do we do when he comes to close out the account?

In real life, it is often not as simple a matter as seeing two different numbers on two different screens. Routinely, data in a database is used in many complex ways. Having two inconsistent balances might mean that a check for $30 bounces, but when we look up the customer's account, it says his balance is $2000. Or worse, a problem might not be readily traceable to a specific number. A report might show that our Baltimore store is losing money at a frightening pace, when in fact it's doing fine, because a purchase for supplies of $10,000 was incorrectly posted as $1 million. But when each individual purchase is examined by the auditor, they're all correct, it's only on the management reports that the incorrect number shows up. That's the kind of database problem that results in stores being closed, money lost, and people losing their jobs.

8.4.3. Aggregate Redundancy

Aggregate redundancy is when one attribute is not identical to another, but can be derived or calculated from several others.

Example 1: A Sale entity includes attributes for sale amount, sales tax rate, and sales tax amount. The sales tax amount is redundant. We could always calculate the tax amount by multiplying the sales tax rate by the sale amount.

Example 2: We have a Sale entity with information about the sale as a whole, and a Sale Item entity with information about individual line items on the sale. So Sale includes attributes like customer and sale date; and Sale Item includes attributes like item number, quantity, and price. Suppose the Sale entity also includes an attribute for total sale amount. This would be redundant, because we could always calculate this by adding up the prices from all the Sale Items.

Example 3: Most examples of aggregate redundancy involve numbers, but they don't have to. Having an attribute for birth date and also for age is redundant, as age can be calculated from birth date and current date. So is having an attribute for full name and also separate attributes for first name and last name.

The problems this causes are the same as for the other types of redundancy. What do we do if the sales tax amount is not equal to the sale price times the tax rate? What does this mean?

8.4.4. Non-Examples

Let me clarify a few cases that may appear to be examples of redundancy, but are not.

(a) References. When we get to discussing the physical model, I'll explain that relationships are implemented by adding "references" or "posted identifiers". If there is a many-to-one relationship between Employee and Department, then each Employee record will have the key of that Employee's department posted into his record. (See section 12.3.) There's nothing mysterious about this: If Bob Smith works for the service department, and we identify the service department as department "102", then we'll have a "Department" attribute in the Employee entity, and for Bob Smith the value will be "102". We then have a "Department ID" in both the Department entity and in the Employee entity. But this is not redundant, because the purpose of this attribute is to tie the two together. If the two records didn't share a common value, there'd be no way to connect them. There's no way the two can be inconsistent or contradict, because the whole point is that we are connecting records with identical values.

(b) Same or similar name but different context. Suppose we have a Sale entity to record things we have sold to our customers, and a Purchase entity to record things we have bought from our suppliers. In both Sale and Purchase there is an attribute of "Price". This is not redundant because it is two different prices: One is the price we paid to buy it and the other is the price we charged when we sold it. We would not expect the two prices to be the same. If we can't charge a higher price for a product when we sell it then we paid to buy it, we're not going to stay in business very long.

(c) Same domain but different values. We could have a Sale entity and a Payment entity that both have a "Transaction Number" attribute. This is not redundant if we never have a Sale with the same transaction number as a Payment. In that case, the two attributes share a common "pool" of values. Such a pool is called a "domain".

That said, if you think you have an example of case (b) or especially (c) you should carefully examine your schema. You may be creating potential redundancy, or you may have redundancy and are just trying to talk yourself out of believing it.

8.5.   Implied Attributes

An "implied attribute" is information that is associated with a specific value of some other attribute, rather than being stored as its own attribute. Avoid implied attributes. You are using implied attributes when you write programs that check for a value in an attribute, and then take action that has nothing to do with the attribute's name or definition.

Adventures
in Real Life!

I was a consultant to a large manufacturing company, working with their human resources system.

At one point the company sold off a division. Of course it was not a matter of simply deleting all the data for people who worked for that division. There was a transition period where employees would still have their health and retirement plans with us even though they were now working for the new company. Data about the sold division still had to be kept for tax purposes. Employees who had retired before the sale would still get their pensions from us. Etc.

Everybody in the HR IT department groaned about all the work they would have to do to support this, going through every program and making modifications. In some cases the sold division would still be processed normally, in others it would be ignored, and in yet others it would be processed slightly differently from other divisions.

The right way to do this would have been to add a "Sold Flag" to the Division entity, true for this division that had been sold, false for all the others. But instead their chief analyst decided that it would be easier to add a check for the specific division number where necessary. So all through dozens of programs, they added places where it said, "if division = '142' ... else ..." Of course this worked and so they thought it was a good solution.

Then about six months later the company sold off another division. I remember sitting in a meeting where one of the programmers whined, "We just did this for Division 142. Now we have to go through it all over again!" And of course they couldn't just search the program text for tests for division 142, because they had been doing this sort of thing for years, putting in tests for specific divisions every time a special case came up.

If they had added the Sold Flag, it would have done little to ease the pain of handling the first sold division. But when the second division was sold, the entire job would have been to change the Sold Flag from false to true. Update one attribute in one record. It would have taken minutes. Instead it took five people several months.

A sure sign that you are using implied attributes is when you compare an attribute to a long list of possible values. When you start writing code like "if foobar = 'A' or foobar = 'C' or foobar = 'F7' or foobar = 'H4' ...", it is likely that foobar has nothing to do with the real condition that you are testing for, but that instead of creating a new attribute to hold what you need, you are figuring out in your program which records would have had the new attribute if you had created it.

The problem with this, as the above story illustrates, is that every time you change the implied association, you have to check every program to see if it should be included in one of these lists. This is a nightmare to be avoided. At best it's a lot of work. At worst you miss a place and get incorrect results. Indeed, just adding a new record to your database might make the existing program invalid: perhaps the new record should be among those checked for special handling.

Doing it right also makes the programs more clear and therefore more maintainable. If I read a line of code that says "if sold_flag == true", it's pretty obvious what the purpose is. But if I read "if division == 142", it is not necessarily clear why that division is special in this particular context.

8.6.   Data Dictionary

As you are collecting attributes, it is often a good idea to create a "data dictionary". This is a list of all the attributes that you have identified, with names, aliases, definitions, size, format, and where applicable, lists of possible values. That is, everything you know about the attribute. It is also handy if you record the sources of your information – who told you or what policy manual it came from – so if there are questions later you know where to look. This can be created as a simple word processing file, or there are products on the market to help you maintain such a dictionary. The data dictionary should be made available to everyone on the design team.

In practice, a data dictionary is normally used intensively during the design process, but once the system is deployed it tends to be neglected. No one ever updates it and no one ever consults it. This is too bad, because a data dictionary can be a very useful tool for programmers trying to maintain the code and designers trying to make updates. If you can keep your data dictionary alive, good for you.

8.7. Attributes and Entity-Relationship Diagrams

It is sometimes useful to show attributes on our ERDs. To do this, in the entity box we draw a line underneath the entity name, and list the attributes beneath this. See Figure 8.1

Another approach is to put attributes in ovals and draw lines from these ovals to the relevant entities. But this takes up a lot of room, and really clutters the chart. It also obscures the fact that each attribute is and can only be associated with a single entity. Designers may be tempted to draw more than one line from a single attribute. I use this notation in Figure 8.2 in the next section, partly to illustrate the technique and partly because it is useful in that special

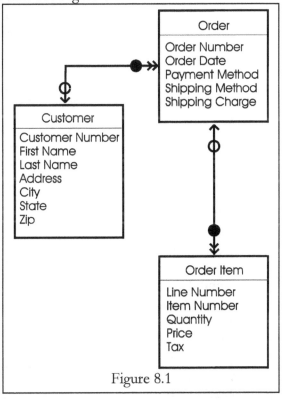

Figure 8.1

case. In a real diagram we would have not one attribute, but usually at least several attributes per entity.

Personally, I rarely include attributes on an ERD. If the database is large, then this makes a diagram that is very large and cluttered and therefore difficult to read. If the database is small, then it's not that hard to comprehend anyway and the effort is largely unnecessary.

On a recent project we had the use of a large-format printer, and so we produced an ERD showing all the attributes that was 5 feet tall and 7 feet wide. This was big enough that even with all the attributes it was readable. We hung it on the wall of my assistant's office and referred to it regularly.

8.8. Attributes with Relationships

Some experts say that relationships can have attributes. Others say that they cannot, that only entities can have attributes.

I side with the "no" votes. If you are tempted to put attributes on a relationship, you can always avoid this by promoting the relationship to an entity, and then connecting the two original entities to this new entity.

For example, suppose you have entities for Voter and Candidate. You want to create a Voter votes-for Candidate relationship. This is M:M, as a Voter can vote for many Candidates -- for different offices and in different elections -- and a Candidate can receive many votes. (If she hopes to win the election, anyway.) You are tempted to attach an attribute of "Election Date" to this relationship, because you need to keep track of which election this vote occurred in.

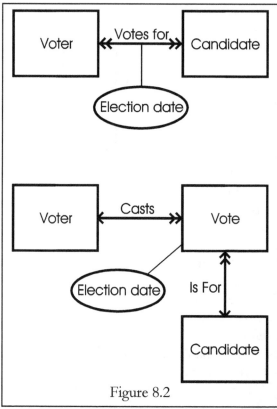

Figure 8.2

An alternative is to create a new entity, let's call it "Vote". Make a 1:M relationship between Voter and Vote and another 1:M relationship between Candidate and Vote. Attach the Election Date attribute to Vote. This gives the same effect as attaching the attribute to the relationship. See Figure 8.2.

On the downside, this turns two entities into three and one relationship into two. But the plus is that we keep each of these things simpler. Adding attributes to relationships make relationships more complicated when it isn't really necessary, because we already have something to hold attributes: entities.

That said, if you find relationship attributes useful and clear, perhaps if you have some unusual situation, don't feel that it is absolutely forbidden. It's just discouraged.

8.9. EAL Notation

We often find it convenient to give a concise list of entities and attributes. A convenient notation is to make a list with one entity per line, each line consisting of the entity name, followed by the attributes in parentheses and separated by commas.

Example:
Customer (customer id, address, city, state, zip)
Sale (receipt number, customer id, store number)
Sale Item (receipt number, item number, price, sales tax)

I don't know any generally-accepted name for this notation. For convenience in this book, I'll call it an "Entity Attribute List", or EAL.

If the list of attributes doesn't fit on one line, this should not create an ambiguity because the end of the list is marked by the closing parenthesis. But to enhance readability, you should use indenting.

The point of EAL is to be concise. It deliberately does not include any information about the size or type of the attributes, that is, it doesn't say whether an attribute is a date or an integer or text or what. Often this will be obvious from the name, but not always. When you need to convey more information … use something else.

We will discuss some further details of EAL in the next chapter.

8.10. Dot Notation

It is often necessary, or at least helpful, to identify the entity to which an attribute belongs. If we simply name the attribute, the entity may not be obvious. In cases where the same attribute name occurs in more than one entity, it may be necessary to specify the entity to avoid ambiguity. Rather than repeatedly writing a long-winded phrase like "the Price attribute of the Purchase entity", a common shorthand is to write the entity name, a period, and the attribute name. For example, "Purchase.Price".

8.11.   Review Questions

1.   What is an attribute?

2.   What are the three parts of the definition of an attribute?

3.   What are the three kinds of redundancy discussed in this chapter?

4.   How do we show attributes on an ERD?

5.   How can we remove attributes from relationships without losing the information?

6.   What is EAL notation?

7.   What is dot notation?

9. KEYS

No one can drive us crazy unless we give them the keys.

-- Doug Horton

9.1. Definition

Every instance of an entity should have a "key" or "identifier". This is some attribute or combination of attributes that is used to identify a record. For example, we may assign each customer a "Customer Number". When we want to retrieve, update, or delete a record, we need a unique identifier to tell the database exactly which record we are talking about.

No ambiguity can be tolerated here. There must be one and only one record with any given key value. When a customer sends us a check, we must to be able to identify exactly which customer it is, or we'll be marking the wrong customer as paid up and sending nasty letters to a customer who has paid. This is terrible for both collections and customer relations.

An entity may have more than one key. Our employees may be uniquely identified by their social security numbers, and also by their employee numbers. We pick one of the available keys to be the "primary key" or "identifier". Sometimes we call all the possible keys "candidate keys", one of which is picked to be the primary key. (This is, unfortunately, slightly different usage from "candidate entity" or "candidate attribute". A candidate entity is a suggestion that may turn out not to be a valid entity at all. But a candidate key is always a key, just maybe not the one we choose for our primary key. There is no generally-accepted term for a suggestion that might be a key.)

A key can be a combination of attributes. Sometimes one attribute by itself is not enough to uniquely identify a record, but some combination of attributes taken together will do the trick. Suppose we have an entity for locations in a warehouse. The combination of row, aisle, and shelf might make a unique key. Any one of these by itself surely would not.

A key must be absolutely guaranteed to be unique. For example, a customer's name would not be usable as a key. We could easily have more than one customer named "Jim Smith" or "Mary Jones". Names of places and organizations can be just as problematic. There are at least 40 towns in the United States named "Springfield". If there is any possibility at all that an attribute is not unique, then it cannot be used as a key.

The guarantee of uniqueness must be 100%: "almost always" doesn't cut it. Database designers often shoot themselves in the foot on this point. They try to put together combinations of attributes that they think will surely be unique. I once saw a customer id made up of customer last name plus zip code plus birth date. The developer no doubt said to himself, What are the odds that we'll get two people with the same values for all three of those things? Surely very, very small. The problem with this is that "very unlikely" is not "impossible". It could happen by coincidence. In this example, it could happen by something that is not a coincidence at all: What about twin brothers both still living in the town of their birth? As long as duplicates are possible, we have the danger that our system will crash or give incorrect results.

9.2. Natural vs Synthetic Keys

So how do we get a unique key? There are two ways:

One, we might find some existing attribute or combination of attributes in our data that meet the uniqueness requirement. That is, there may be attributes that we needed anyway that also make a candidate key. This is called a "natural key". For example, a payroll system almost certainly needs to hold every employee's Social Security Number so we can report tax information to the government. An SSN is guaranteed to be unique, so this would be a natural key.

Two, we might create an attribute whose only purpose is to serve as a key. If we create it, we can invent some system to insure that it will be unique. This is called a "synthetic key", "object identifier", or "abstract identifier". In this book we will use the term "synthetic key". The simplest thing to do is create a sequence number: the first record entered is #1, the second is #2, and so on. Sometimes more complex schemes are devised, like having separate sequences within a department or category. In such cases the textbook correct thing to do is to break the category and the sequence number into separate attributes. Otherwise we would be breaking the "one fact per field" rule. See section 8.3. However, this can be inconvenient, so often they are kept together, or the category is duplicated. See section 16.4.

A synthetic key may be presented to the user. For example we often create synthetic keys to identify a customer, and then print this on statements as an "Account Number". Or the synthetic key may be entirely behind the scenes. The database and programming may use it to connect records and hold references without ever displaying it to the user.

A natural key must be entered by the user as, by definition, it is *not* generated by the system. If the user is going to enter it we will probably make it visible to him later.

To put it another way, a natural key exists in the "real world" outside of our system, while a synthetic key only exists within the system. When we way that a natural key exists in the real world, we mean the real world of the users of our system, not necessarily of normal human beings. For example, the IRS assigns an "Employer Identification Number" to every business in the country. Most people probably don't know what an EIN is, but to a computer system, it's a natural key.

Something that is a synthetic key in one system may be a natural key in another. Employer Identification Number is a synthetic key to the Internal Revenue Service – they generate them essentially as a sequence number. But to most computer systems in the world, it's a natural key, because they get it from outside the system. If you're not sure whether a key is natural or synthetic, just ask one question: Is it generated by this system, or is it typed in by the user or imported from some other system? If it's system-generated, it's synthetic. If it's from outside, it's natural.

There is a great deal of debate among database designers on whether natural keys or synthetic keys are better. Let's try to fairly discuss the arguments for each side.

9.2.1. Advantages of Synthetic Keys

1. Unique: The essential requirement for any key is that it must be 100% guaranteed to be unique. This requirement is easily met with a synthetic key: If we invent the key as we go along, we can always pick a value that we have never used before. If we use a sequence number, we just take the next available number.

Guaranteeing uniqueness is often a problem for natural keys. As I noted earlier, names – whether of people, places, organizations, or whatever – rarely give much assurance of uniqueness. By definition, a natural key is defined outside our system. Therefore, by definition we have no control over how it is assigned and we cannot ourselves guarantee anything about it.

2. Short: A synthetic key can be a single, short attribute. A natural key is often fairly long. Sometimes it takes several attributes combined to make a useable natural key. A common choice for a synthetic key is a 4-byte integer sequence number. That allows us to count to over 2 billion. Even allowing for high turnover, it is rare for any entity to have over 2 billion records. If we really have over 2 billion customers, we can afford to buy a bigger disk drive and use an 8-byte integer, which allows us to count to 9 quintillion (9×10^{18}). Either way, that's shorter than a natural key is likely to be, which will make indexes smaller and faster. Because it's a single attribute, programming is simpler: we only have to manipulate one attribute at a time instead of several.

3. Simple: We can use synthetic keys consistently to simplify the design of the system: We decide once that all tables will have a

synthetic key meeting certain conditions. Like, we may say that it is always a 4-byte integer sequence number, and it is always named after the table followed by "_id", like "customer_id" or "product_id". Then a programmer looking at any table automatically knows what the key is.

4. Immutable: A synthetic key can be declared immutable. That is, once assigned, it will never change. Natural keys can rarely offer this guarantee. If we used, say, a customer's phone number as the key to our customer table, a customer might move and get a new phone number, or the phone company may create a new area code and change his number. Even for values that are not supposed to change, like a social security number, as they must be entered by a user, we must allow for the possibility that the user made a mistake keying them in and so there must be a way to correct them. Immutability means that we do not need to write code to handle changes in key values. Being able to process such changes in a reasonable amount of time sometimes means that we need to create indexes whose only purpose is to support changing keys, which can bog down system performance. And if our code to process key changes has errors, we can find ourselves with corrupted data.

9.2.2. Advantages of Natural Keys

1. Familiar: We usually need to include natural keys in the system because they're important to the user, regardless of whether we actually use them as keys. We probably need to include an employee's social security number, and we surely need to include his name.

2. Non-redundant: Often the user thinks of the natural key as the identifier. If a synthetic key is displayed for the user, this can seem redundant and confusing. Like, why does every part have both a "part number" and a "part identifier"? If it is not displayed, it can be mysterious. How come the same part number shows up twice -- I thought that was the key?

3. Readable: When a programmer or database designer is examining the database, it is a lot easier to read the data if it uses natural keys. By definition these are meaningful values, rather than seemingly-random numbers. Ad hoc queries are easier to construct and comprehend.

4. Re-discoverable: If the database is corrupted, there is much more hope of repairing the damage when it uses natural keys. For example, suppose we have a database that includes entities for

Customers and Orders. Order records are connected to a Customer by posting the key of the Customer record in the Order record. One day a hundred customer records are lost – whether because of a programming error, hardware failure, or whatever. If we used a natural key, say the customer's phone number, there would be some hope of repairing the damage. We could look at phone numbers in the Order records, look those numbers up in the phone book, and not only would we then know who the lost customers are, but we would also know which Order went with each Customer. But suppose instead we used a synthetic key for the Customer entity. Then the Customer key posted in each order record would just be a meaningless number. Not only would we have no clue who the lost customers were, but even if we somehow discovered who they were, we would still have to figure out how to connect the right Orders to each Customer. Note that this example is not contrived: The definition of a natural key is that it exists outside our system, so there is often an outside source to look up and validate these keys.

5. Mnemonic: In some cases, a natural key may be mnemonic. That is, it may be something that the user can remember, like a code or abbreviation. A synthetic key will never be mnemonic.

6. Self-sufficient: A natural key may reduce the number of joins between entities that we have to do. Suppose we have an Office entity and a Sale entity. There is a many-to-one relationship between Sale and Office: Sale is-made-by Office. Thus, we post the key of Office into Sale. A likely query would be to find the total dollar sales for each office for a given time period.

If we use a natural key for Office, then the query could be simply:

```
select office_code, sum(amount)
from sale
group by office_code
order by office_code
```

As office_code is a natural key that is familiar to the users, then it is sufficient to identify the Office to them, and in many cases this will be sufficient for display. Everything we need is in one entity.

But if we have a synthetic key that is not familiar to the users, then we must do something more like:

```
select office.office_code, sum(sale.amount)
from office join sale using (office_id)
group by office_code
order by office_code
```

We must use the "internal" identifier from Sale to find the corresponding Office so that we can retrieve an "external" identifier that is meaningful to the users for display. The only reason to read the Office record is to get a user-meaningful identifier. We must read an additional entity just to translate the identifier to something meaningful. In complex queries this can add many more tables. It makes queries harder to read and slower to run.

9.2.3. Hazy Cases

There are two important types of keys that are not clearly either natural or synthetic. There are no generally accepted terms for these in the industry, so I will call them "assigned codes" and "base sequences".

9.2.4. Assigned Codes

The user may be required to invent a unique identifier for each new record as it is added. That is, we don't use an existing identifier, nor does the system create one. Instead, the user creates one when needed. The system checks that the selected value is not already being used. If it is, it requires the user to try again.

The main reason for using an assigned code is to get a mnemonic key when no natural key exists.

If you're reading this book, you probably have an email address. This is an example of an assigned code. You are typically asked what email address you want. You likely pick your name or a nickname, or maybe a job title. If someone else has already picked that email address, you are required to make another choice.

I often use assigned codes for frequently-used lookup tables. Suppose in our database we record merchandise sold in our store. We attach a category to various types of merchandise: men's clothes, women's clothes, appliances, cleaning products, etc. It makes sense to have a short code for each of these categories. Not only is this more efficient for the system, but the user probably prefers a short abbreviation also. It is surely easier, when typing in a list of the products that arrived in today's shipment, to just type "JCL" rather than "junior girls' clothes" or "APL" rather than "automotive parts – lubricants". But this works best if the code is at least reasonably mnemonic. If the user has to type 324092 for junior girls' clothes and 23902309 for automotive parts – lubricants, that is not very convenient at all. And the easiest way to make codes that the user considers rational and easy to remember is to let the user make them up herself. Then all the system has to do is block attempts to create duplicates.

From the system's point of view, assigned codes have most of the advantages of natural keys: They are readable and mnemonic. They are somewhat familiar and possibly self-sufficient.

Like synthetic keys, they are guaranteed to be unique and can be short and simple.

9.2.5. Base Sequences

Developers sometimes create a key using an existing attribute that is known to not be unique, the "base", and then add a sequence number to it. For example, a person might be identified by his last name, plus a sequence number to distinguish anyone who happens to have the same last name. So the first Smith goes in as SMITH or SMITH1, the next Smith as SMITH2, etc. If the base is usually unique, then most key values are simply the base value.

A base sequence is system-generated, but from a value entered by the user.

Depending on how you look at it, such a key either combines the best features of both natural and synthetic keys, or it combines all the worst.

The sequence number guarantees that it is unique. The base will offer at least some of the advantages of being readable, rediscoverable, and mnemonic.

To achieve the shortness objective, if the base is potentially long we may truncate it. Instead of using the customer's full name, we just use the first three or four letters. As the sequence number guarantees uniqueness, it doesn't hurt anything to truncate it.

On the other hand, a base sequence usually cannot be stored as an integer, which hurts efficiency. Generating the sequence number is more complex than for a synthetic key because it has to be referenced against the base attribute. While it is based on an existing attribute, it is not an existing attribute, so it is only partially familiar to the user.

9.2.6. Opinions

Database designers argue back and forth. As you gain experience, you'll come to your own conclusions. But for what it's worth, here are mine.

I generally prefer natural keys. When there is no good natural key available, I do not force it: For entities with few records, I use assigned codes. For entities with many records, I use a synthetic key. The reason for the difference is that for codes that are used regularly, it is handy to the user to have a mnemonic value. But for records in big entities it is usually more of a pain to assign them and to have to resolve duplicates then to just accept a sequence number. If you require the user to make up a key for every customer, they're going to get very annoyed trying to find an unused value for the latest Smith. They'll probably end up numbering them anyway, or each clerk will have a different scheme and we'll end up with a messy hash.

I've used base sequences on occasion, but I usually regretted it later as offering no clear advantages.

I decidedly avoid natural keys constructed out of many pieces of unrelated data, like "first three letters of last name plus store number of first contact plus blood type". These are a product of desperation. If there's no good, obvious natural key, use a synthetic key or an assigned code.

9.3. Primary Key

We must pick one key for an entity as its "primary key". This is the key which is used to identify individual instances of the entity internally. In chapter 11, the Physical Model, we will discuss how we use the primary key in practice. For now, just accept that we will use it in general as an identifier.

If you have only one key, then it is the primary key", because it's the only candidate around. If you have more than one key, pick one. Because we are going to use this to identify records, it is convenient to use the shortest key available. Especially, a primary key that is only one attribute is generally preferred over one that is multiple attributes, because it will be simpler to work with. If lengths and attribute counts are similar, pick the one that is most obvious, familiar, or generally used. If no key is clearly better than the others by these criteria, then it doesn't matter: just pick one.

9.4. Keys and Defining Relationships

When an entity is related to another with a defining relationship, there is normally a candidate key consisting of a key of the parent entity plus one (or more) additional attributes.

Example: In our customer order database, there is a 1:M defining relationship between Customer and Order, and another 1:M defining relationship between Order and Line Item. The key of Customer is Customer Number. A likely key for Order is Customer Number plus Order Number. A likely key for Line Item is then Customer Number plus Order Number plus Line Number.

These keys may or may not be the primary key. If we are using synthetic keys for the primary keys, these would not be the primary keys.

9.5. ERDs and EALs

In chapter 7 we learned about Entity-Relationship Diagrams (ERDs) and in chapter 8 Entity-Attribute Lists (EALs). Now that you know about keys, let us add two details.

First, we want to identify the attributes that make up the primary key. The same techniques are used on both ERDs and EALs, though no one can agree on exactly what those techniques are. Some experts say you should underline these attributes, others that you should write them in italics, or put an asterisk (*) after their names, or write "(PK)" for "primary key". In this book I will use the asterisk notation, because it is concise and works regardless of font or word processing software.

Second, it is often necessary to put the primary key of one entity into another in order to connect them. We will discuss this in detail in chapter 11, the Physical Model. We want to identify attributes used this way also. Again, a variety of notational conventions are used. Some put a caret (^) or other punctuation after the name, others write "(FK)" for "foreign key". In this book, I will use a caret.

EAL Example:

Customer (customer id*, address, city, state, zip)
Sale (receipt number*, customer id^, store number^)
Sale Item (sale item id*,receipt number^, item number^, price, sales tax)

The same attribute could be both part of a primary key and a foreign key. An example is defining relationships. If the primary key of Order is Customer Number plus Order Number, then Customer Number is both a foreign key and part of the primary key. In that case we use both symbols, like "customer number*^" or "customer number (pk,fk)".

We do not normally identify keys other than the primary key in an EAL or ERD.

9.6. Review Questions

1. What is a key? What is the one absolute requirement for a key?

2. What is the difference between a natural key and a synthetic key. List four advantages of a synthetic key and six advantages of a natural key.

3. What is a "primary key"? What makes a good choice for a primary key?

10. NAMES

Now the LORD God had formed out of the ground all the beasts of the field and all the birds of the air. He brought them to the man to see what he would name them; and whatever the man called each living creature, that was its name.

-- Genesis 2:19 (NIV)

10.1.   Importance

When designing a database, we have to make up names for entities, attributes, and sometimes relationships. Once you have created a database, it is very difficult to change names later. You could have dozens or hundreds of programs using these names, scattered across many systems. You are going to be living with any names you invent for a long time to come, so it's worth putting a little thought into them.

10.2. Format

For the logical and physical models, we do not need to worry about the format of names. That is, names can be any length, may include spaces and punctuation, and so on. This will not be true when we get to the implementation, where the database language will have specific rules about length and character set and reserved words.

But let's not abuse our freedom here. While there's nothing to stop us from naming an attribute "!!Hoolah 42?#%$whAM", that is probably not a good idea. Names should generally be limited to capital and small letters, spaces, and an occasional hyphen or some digits.

10.3. Good Names

At the very least, an adequate name is mnemonic, that is, when you learn once what the name represents, you can remember it. Even a highly abbreviated name can do this. If you see an attribute name of "avgdayprec", it may be hard to guess what that holds. But if you are told that it stands for "average daily precipitation", it shouldn't be hard to remember what that name means when you see it again.

A good name is one that is not only mnemonic, but gives strong clues what it means. "average daily precipitation" would be a good attribute name, though admittedly long. We may abbreviate this if the abbreviations are likely to be familiar to anyone who would look at our schema. Presumably anyone looking at this system will know or quickly figure out that it includes meteorological information, so "avg daily precip" would probably be adequately explanatory.

More specifically, names should be descriptive, precise, concise, and consistent.

10.4. Descriptive

A name should tell us what this object is. This may sound obvious, but is ignored surprisingly often. The most common reason is laziness: A designer uses some very short, meaningless name because it is easy to type and doesn't require thought. The extreme case of this is when someone gives names like "N1", "N2", etc.

Adventures
in Real Life!

Our customer entity had an attribute called "sex code". I was expecting this to be a one position alpha with values like "M" and "F". But when I looked at the data, it turned out to be two position numeric, like "11" and "37". I was beginning to wonder if it was not "which" but "how often". On further investigation I found a list of code values. 01 = Mr, 02 = Mrs, 03 = Miss, 04 = Ms, 05 = Dr, 06 = Lt Col, and so on. We had customers in Europe so the list included Baron and Earl.

So it was not really a "sex code" at all, but rather a "courtesy title code". The attribute was confusing because it had a misleading name.

Use names that accurately describe the object.

Some designers include a data type or kind as part of every attribute name.

"Type" here means text, number, Boolean, date, maybe a few others.

"Kind" means a role that the data performs, like count, amount, name, description, flag, etc. Kinds are less strictly defined than types.

When I write "type or kind" I mean that some designers believe you should include a type, others believe you should include a kind.

Sometimes the data type or kind is so obvious that specifying it seems rather superfluous. We do not gain much by calling an attribute "Customer Address Text" rather than "Customer Address". Surely no one is likely to suppose that "Customer Address" is a date or a Boolean. But in other cases it conveys valuable information. "Hire Date" is not at all redundant. "Hire" by itself could be a flag indicating whether we want to hire this person, it could be text describing the job we want to hire him for, or various other possibilities.

It's a no-brainer that you should include a type or kind when it clearly helps identify what this attribute is. Those who say to always include it say that when in doubt, it is better to give the extra information, and even when it adds nothing, it is better to be consistent.

Personally, I rarely include a type or kind in an attribute name when it is not obviously necessary for clarity, but I think it's an idea that has a lot of merit. The main drawback is that it is awkward.

I think a kind is more useful than a type, because a kind tells us more. The idea of a kind is that it tells us what the data is for, while a type simply tells us what it looks like. Also, a kind is more permanent. The more specific a type is, the less permanent it is. For example, some distinguish a short integer from a long integer in their attribute names. But we might initially create an attribute as a short and later discover that occasionally we need to hold bigger numbers, so we change it to a long. Having to rename the attribute through dozens or hundreds of programs because of a size change is tedious.

10.5.   Precise

A name must be as precise as is necessary to distinguish it from any other name we are using.

In conventional English, when we want to describe something we typically give one or more adjectives followed by a noun. For example "large green chair". This clearly identifies it as a chair but distinguishes it from red chairs of any size or small chairs of any color.

When two attributes or entities are similar, give them names that are similar enough to show the connection, but give at least a hint what is different. That is, include words in the name that indicate what the larger group or idea is, and additional words that express the difference.

Suppose you need to keep track of both state and federal income tax. You create attributes to hold these amounts. Good names would be "State Income Tax" and "Federal Income Tax". This clearly identifies what they have in common – "income" and "tax" – while distinguishing one as "state" and one as "federal". Designers often fail to clearly identify the difference. "State Tax" and "Income Tax" would be poor choices, because they fail to make clear that the former is also an income tax and the latter is federal. Someone reading our list of attributes later could be forgiven for supposing that perhaps the first is a sales tax or that the second is a state income tax.

Avoid using numbers to distinguish two similar attributes. If you are tempted to name two attributes "Balance 1" and "Balance 2", consider the person who will have to figure out the difference later. Why are there two balances? What is really different between them?

Surely you can give more helpful information. If one is the balance before posting this month's payment and the other is the balance after, then call them "Balance Before Payment" and "Balance After Payment".

Avoid differences in names that give no clue about the differences in data. I used to work on a system for medical office billing that had several reports that included each patient's balance due and a total for all patients. The programmer before me called the patient's total balance "chgtot" and the grand total "totchg". Or maybe it was the other way around. "Patient Total" and "Grand Total" would have been more helpful. Even if he insisted on abbreviating them to "pattot" and "grandtot", I could have remembered which was which. I've seen many systems where a database designer used a different abbreviation of a name or even deliberately misspelled a name just to make it different from another similar object. Like, he'll call one attribute "Amount Pd" and another "Amt Paid", or call one table "Customer" and another "Customerr". (Doubling the last letter or changing a vowel are common tactics.)

Such techniques are maddeningly uninformative. If you're creating two objects instead of one, it must be because there is something different between them. Tell me what that difference is. You don't have to tell me everything there is to know about the difference. Just give me hint.

10.6. Concise

Avoid making names longer than necessary to be descriptive and precise. Some developers react to excessively short names by making names that are too long.

Long names are, simply, a pain. No one wants to type or write "amount paid by the customer as payment against his or her outstanding balance" over and over. It's just tiresome and a waste of time.

Long names also make it more difficult to clearly know whether we are talking about the same or a different thing. When we want to know whether the attribute mentioned in the email from Bob is the same as the attribute discussed in the requirements document, of course we have to compare the names. The longer the name, the more text there is to compare. If we have long names that are very similar, it's easy to see someone getting confused between "amount paid by the customer as payment against his or her outstanding balance" and "amount paid for the customer as payment against his or her outstanding balance". Did you see the difference between those two names instantly or did you have to look over them a couple of times?

We can identify a few specific rules for keeping names concise.

One: Don't include words like "entity", "field", or any other words identifying what kind of object this names. That is, don't call an entity "customer entity", just call it "customer". I once saw a list of attributes where every name began "attribute containing".

Two: Avoid using prepositions or other connecting words. Rearrange the words if necessary to make the name clear without these. For example, don't call an attribute "payment made by customer". Just call it "customer payment". Don't call it "date of birth", just "birth date". We are writing a title, not a sentence.

Three: Leave out words that do not clarify or restrict the meaning. Anything else is redundant or superfluous. Consider "customer order date". Do we have orders other than orders from customers? If not, then the word "customer" is unnecessary, and we should call it simply "order date".

Some experts say that an attribute name should be understood within the context of its entity. Others say an attribute name should stand on its own. Suppose we have a Sale entity that has an attribute for the date the sale was made. By the stand-alone philosophy, we might call this attribute "sale date". By the context philosophy, we could call it simply "date".

The implication of the context philosophy is that we will often have attributes in different entities with the same name. We might have a "date" attribute in Sale, in Shipment, in Stock Transfer, and many other entities. We will have many attributes scattered across many entities with names like "amount", "name", "code", and other general terms. Advocates of this system say that this is no problem, because if there is any ambiguity, we just express the name with dot notation: it's "Customer.Name" or "Vendor.Name" or "Product.Name".

While I don't want to be dogmatic on the subject, I dislike the context philosophy for two reasons.

One, attributes used as foreign keys often must have different names in their "home" entity than they have in the referencing table. Especially if we use synthetic keys, we could have many entities with an attribute called "id". When, say, the Employee entity references the Department entity, we can't call the posted foreign key "id", because here that refers to the Employee id. This would not only be confusing but would create two attributes with the same name. So we end up calling it "id" in Department but "department_id" anywhere else. Or worse, it's called "id" in Department and "division number" in Employee.

Two, overly simple names set us up for problems when new attributes must be added later. Suppose we call the sale date in our Sale entity simply "date". A year after we deploy version one we make a change to the system to add delivery information, so now we need a "deliver date". So now we have "date" and "deliver date". This fails the precision test.

"NEVER USE A LONG WORD WHEN A DIMINUTIVE ONE WILL DO."

10.7. Consistent

Keep your names consistent.

Your English teacher may have told you to avoid using the same word repeatedly because it can sound tedious and awkward. Instead they tell you to switch among synonyms. "Jack drove his car to the car dealer and parked next to a red car" sounds very repetitive. Better to write, "Jack drove his car to the auto dealer and parked next to a red vehicle."

But when naming database objects, you should not use any synonyms. Pick one word for each idea and use it consistently. Yes, this is boring. But it is clear and unambiguous.

In the narrowest sense, this means that when the same attribute occurs in more than one entity, you should give it the same name.

 Adventures in Real Life!

A retail system had the product cost and shipping cost information in the Product entity. When an item was added to the warehouse, these costs were copied to the Stock entity. This was not redundant data because the Product entity held the current costs, while the Stock entity held the costs at the time that particular unit was purchased. When the price from the company's suppliers changed, they had to remember what they had actually paid for the stock already bought. These values were also copied into the Sale Item entity when the item was sold, which was redundant, but not the point here.

So all well and good, except that in the Product entity these attributes were called "unitcost" and "freight", in the Stock entity they were called "cost" and "freightcost", and in the Sale Item entity they were called "unitcost" and "shippingcost". When I first looked at this database, it was not at all obvious that these things were the same.

More generally, use consistent terminology. Don't name one attribute "Product Name" and another "Item Vendor" if "product" and "item" are two words for the same idea. Don't call it a "price" over here and an "amount" over there. Etc.

Use consistent abbreviations. If you abbreviate account as "acct", fine, just use that same abbreviation everywhere. If you have many abbreviations, make a list of them and post it somewhere for all the members of the development team.

You can give your entities plural names, like "Customers" and "Products", or you can give them singular names, like "Customer" and "Product". But don't mix the two. Don't call them "Customers" and "Product".

Sometimes the users have more than one name for something. As database designers, our job is to fight this. We should pick one name that we then use consistently. Other names should be carefully recorded and filed as "aliases". We want to remember aliases so that when this name comes up again as we do further research, we can relate it to the name that we have decided to use. But we don't want to use it ourselves: We should always translate to the consistent name. We may have to concede as far as putting both names on screens or reports so that users familiar with the name we decided not to use will not be confused. But try to move the users toward a single, consistent name.

10.8. Local Terminology

Whenever possible, use terminology familiar to your users' organization. Do not substitute terminology from other organizations you have worked with in the past or try to replace their specialized terms with common speech. It will only confuse everyone.

For example, if your user organization refers to a customer as a "client", call the table "Client", not "Customer".

However, if the users' terminology causes problems, sometimes you must confront this and pressure the users to change their terminology. This can be a difficult decision. If your users have a word that has a common meaning very different from the way they are using it, this is not necessarily a problem. Every profession has technical jargon and every organization has "local dialect" that is special to them. People rarely have difficulty keeping track of the meaning of a word in context. (When the hostess at the restaurant says, "Let me show you to your table," do you get confused, and think that she's talking about a database schema?) Only when the customer's terminology is ambiguous or misleading should the database designer try to change it.

Adventures
in Real Life!

I spent a number of years working on a system that managed technical manuals for the military. An important feature was that users could "requisition" a technical manual, that is, request that a copy be sent now; or users could "subscribe", meaning that they wanted to get any updates to that manual that may be published in the future. Collectively, both of these things were called "requisitions". That is, there were two kinds of "requisitions", one of which was a "requisition". This created an obvious ambiguity, so in the system I insisted on referring to the two types as "subscription" and "one-time". This was a long hard battle as old-timers continued to use the old terms, but I slowly and gradually changed people's language.

On the other hand, sometimes the users will just accept whatever terminology you invent for the database.

Adventures
in Real Life!

In a medical office system, we included an anti-piracy feature where we generated a code number based on the user's name and address as entered in the system, and then the user had to call our office to get a password that would work with this code number. (The idea was that if they tried to give copies to their friends, it wouldn't work.) On the screen this code number was labeled "JFN Code". New users would call in when they got the message asking for a password. Our help desk people would ask them what the JFN code displayed on the screen was and then give them a password. In five years no one ever asked me why it was called a "JFN code". JFN stood for "Johansen's Funny Number".

10.9.   The Of Language

There have been a number of schemes proposed over the years for standardizing the construction of names, especially attribute names. One fairly well-known and standardized technique is the Of Language. It was invented by a team at IBM lead by Ken Orr.

In the Of Language, every attribute name follows a specific format:

```
kind.noun connector modifier ...
```

"kind" is a one-character code for the data type, chosen from the following list:

A	amount
C	code
D	date
F	flag
K	constant
N	name
O	number
P	percent
Q	quantity
T	text
X	control

This is followed by a period, which is read "of". Then is a noun that describes the attribute in general.

This is then followed by zero or more qualifiers, each consisting of a connector and a word that narrows the definition.

The connectors are:

.	of
/	which is (are)
$	or
#	and
@	by, per, for, or with

Qualifiers are arranged in order of increasing specificity. That is, we start with the most general terms and work our way to the most specific.

Examples:

d.birth = date of birth
q.stock/onhand = quantity of stock which is on-hand
a.tax/state$federal = amount of tax which is state or federal
o.vehichles/cars/sedans/fourdoor = number of vehicles which are cars which are sedans which are four-door.

Advantages to the Of Language include:
The data kind of every attribute is clearly identified in its name. For example, if we called the attribute for an employee's state of birth simply "birth", a reader could be forgiven for assuming it was the birth date.

It encourages us to create names that clearly identify what attributes have in common and how they differ.

If we produce a list of attribute names in alphabetical order, related attributes will be next to each other. For example, "n.employee/active" will be right next to "n.employee/retired" and "n.employee/terminated". This can make review of attribute lists more convenient.

But the Of Language also has some troubling disadvantages.
The use of punctuation symbols for the "connectors" may be compact but it takes some practice to learn to read. Few if any database products and computer languages accept such characters as part of an attribute name, at least not without awkward extra coding. Developers typically get around this problem by replacing all the funny characters with underscores or some other character acceptable to the language.

The biggest problem is that Of Language names are simply awkward for English-speaking people to read. They are typically backwards from what we are used to. In English we normally put adjectives or other modifiers first, then the noun, and any kind at the end. But the Of Language does this exactly the other way around. For example, in natural English we might call something "state income tax amount". In the Of Language we would call it "a.tax/income@state", that is "amount of tax which is income for state".

While the Of Language is an intriguing idea, when I have seen organizations try to use it, the effort always seems to fizzle. It's just too unnatural. In my opinion, it's a good basic idea but it needs some serious rework.

But note that most of the advantages can be achieved by application of the principles we discussed earlier in this chapter. While the Of Language might have you call an attribute "c.material/raw", by the rules in this chapter you would call it "raw material code". This conveys the same information but is much more readable and natural.

10.10. Systematic versus Meaningful

Sometimes computer people say that it's a waste of time trying to make a name meaningful, because there's no way we're going to make a name that will instantly tell anyone who sees it exactly what this attribute (or whatever) is.

Usually they go on to argue for a rigid, systematic naming convention. These folks will insist that names should be constructed according to some formula. These schemes usually involve building various codes into the name and ending up with a sequence number.

 Adventures in Real Life!

At my very first computer job, the company introduced a new scheme for naming programs:

The first character identified the communications system used in those pre-Internet days: "I" for IMS, "C" for CICS, or "N" for none.

The second character was "B" for batch or "O" for on-line.

The third identified the language: "C" for COBOL, "P" for PL/1, "A" for assembler, etc.

Then came a four digit sequence number to make the name unique.

The eighth character was "P" for production or "T" for test.

So the first program I worked on under the new system was named "NBC1057P".

The programmers complained that it was impossible to remember what a program did with these cryptic names. The group that devised this naming scheme replied that, as program names then were limited to eight characters, it was impossible to be very meaningful in eight characters. So we would have to keep a list somewhere anyway.

But surely one could convey more meaning than "NBC1057P".

It is, of course, true, that a name of reasonable length cannot describe exactly what a program does or what an attribute contains. But making a name that tells you all there is to know about the object is not necessary. It is sufficient for the name to be mnemonic. If I have to make a change to the program that prints customer statements, of course I would have a hard time guessing what the name of that program is. But if I see that there are programs out there named "PAYCHKS", "INVOICES", "QTRLYTAX", "CUSTSTMT", and "PROFTSHR", and "SALESAUD", which of those do you think might be it? Suppose instead that the list of program names was "NBC1057P", "NBA0972P", "COA0428P", etc. Which list would be easier to work with?

These days the argument that system limits on the length of a name make meaningful names impossible is pretty much obsolete. Most computer systems allow names to be fairly long, usually at least 16 characters, and 32 is common. The limit these days is more how much people are willing to type than what the system allows.

On the other hand, I am hard pressed to think of any advantage to a "systematic" name. In the NBC1057P example I gave above, at one point I was told that the reason for the language code in the name was because the head of the IT department wanted to produce a one-shot report listing the number of programs we had in each language, so he'd know what skills to look for when hiring new people. So, to support this one-time report we're going to condemn ourselves to meaningless names for the rest of our lives?

At another company I was told that they required cryptic file names so that if hackers broke into their system, they wouldn't be able to figure out which files contained data worth stealing. Maybe, I suppose, though that assumes the hackers couldn't just download everything and sort through it at their leisure, and that someone smart enough to break through their security system would be too dumb to use a search program to look for strings in the format of a credit card number or chemical names that would indicate secret formulas. It did mean that their own staff had a hard time finding the data they needed, day after day. They said employees should keep a paper list of what each file contained. But what if thieves broke into the building? Shouldn't all paper files be kept in code to protect against that possibility? The reasoning seemed to be, Yes, our employees can't find the information they need to do their jobs. But spies and hackers can't find the information either, so the system is working!

10.11. Review Questions

1. What are some pros and cons of including a data type in all attribute names?

2. What do we mean when we say a name should be "precise"?

3. What is the difference between the "stand alone" approach to attribute names and the "context" approach?

4. What do we mean when we say your names should be "consistent"?

5. What is the "Of Language"? What are its advantages and disadvantages?

6. What is wrong with systematic names?

11. REQUIREMENTS

Human requirements are the inspiration for art.

-- Stephen Gardiner

11.1. The Problem

We've been discussing how to translate the real-world requirements for your organization into a database model. But this all assumes you know what the requirements are. How do you find out?

Occasionally, you simply know. Perhaps you are both the owner of the company and the database designer. But this is rare. Usually, you have to talk to the people who know the business, read policy manuals, study legal requirements, etc. We collectively refer to these sources as "users".

Users may or may not know anything about database design. Usually they know little or nothing about computers or databases. And this immediately presents a problem. It would be very convenient if we could just ask the users, "What entities, relationships, and attributes do you need in this database?" and they would tell us. But of course their most likely response would be a blank stare, and any answer they did attempt to give us would likely be wildly wrong.

If users could design databases on their own, they wouldn't need you, the database designer, and there would go your big-bucks job. While I say that whimsically, I do have a serious point. Suppose you are tasked to design a database to help meteorologists make weather predictions. The meteorologists you work with may well be highly skilled, very intelligent people. But they have spent their lives learning about meteorology – not about computers. It is hardly realistic to expect them to be experts on computers as well as on meteorology. That is your job.

The problem is how to coax the information we need out of the users. This is called "requirements gathering".

11.2. Identify the Application

The first step is to find out what the users want the new system to do. It's pointless to search for an answer until you know the question. There is the obvious high-level description: Do they want a payroll system? A system to monitor weather patterns? Schedule truck routes? etc. You're not going to get far if you don't even know what the subject is. But beyond that, what is it they want this system to actually do? It's one thing to say, "We want to schedule delivery routes." What does that mean? What information do they expect to give to the system, and what results do they expect it to give back?

11.3. Existing Processes

Unless the organization is getting in to a whole new field, there is some existing process that this database system will replace. Let's assume for the moment that we are replacing a manual or ad hoc process.

Perhaps the users are currently doing the job with pencil and paper. Perhaps they are using ad hoc automation like spreadsheets and word processing files. Perhaps they are using an older computer system – a "legacy system" -- that you are expected to replace.

The users may even say that at present there is no system at all. That is almost certainly not true. They're getting the job done now somehow. The system may be that they scribble it in crayon on a napkin. It may be that the boss relies on his intuition. But they have some way they're doing the job now. Find out what that is.

11.4.   Automation and Re-Engineering

There are two directions to go from there. One is to directly automate the existing process. The other is to re-engineer it.

By "directly automate the existing process", I mean that you may be able to take the existing forms, procedures, calculations, whatever, and put them on a computer. For example, if there is a form the users presently fill out on paper, maybe you can make a Web page that resembles that paper form. If the users are presently adding up a column of numbers, maybe the computer can add it up for them. If in the manual process, the clerk fills out a form and passes it to his supervisor who in turn passes it to the regional manager, maybe you can have the computer system send the information by email or have a "work queue" for each person that information is routed to.

Often some or all of the process should be "re-engineered". That is, there are likely important parts of the process that were needed because of limitations of manual or ad hoc systems, but which are unnecessary or detrimental in a fully-automated system.

An obvious example: On paper forms, it is often necessary to require people to enter the same information on multiple forms. We might need name, address, and phone number on many forms. But on a computer system, asking people to re-enter this information is pointless. Once we collect it once, we can just remember it. Maybe we display it every time and ask the user to confirm.

In database terms, this means that paper forms are inherently unnormalized. It makes sense to repeat information between forms so we don't have to constantly cross-reference other forms. But in an electronic database, a cross-reference is quick and easy.

Adventures in Real Life!

I consulted to a military agency that ran a requisition messaging system.

In the old paper days, a base sent a paper requisition form to a central clearing house. Clerks there looked up the part number requested and some other details in a big book to see what warehouses stocked that item, pick the one closest to the base requesting it, and forward the requisition to that warehouse. Of course the book was always out of date, so the clerks kept a list of "exceptions", and they double-checked every routing against this list. When the book was updated, they threw the exception list away and started a new one.

Then the system was automated. Instead of mailing in a paper form, the message was sent electronically. The computer automatically looked up the part number in the routing table and forwarded the message to the warehouse. A process that used to take days in the mail and days more on a clerk's desk now took seconds.

Except ... instead of maintaining a single routing file, they continued the idea of having a routing book and an exception list. The program first looked up each requisition in the routing file. Then it looked it up in the exception file. If no record was found there, it routed the requisition based on the routing file. If it found an exception record, it routed by that.

It made sense to have two lists when it was done on paper. It took time to print a new book. Changes had to be accumulated, type set (remember this was pre-word processor days), proof copies reviewed, and finally a print run scheduled. So you needed a temporary list while you waited for all this to happen.

But on a computer system, it would have been just as easy to update the routing file as to update the exception file. What was gained by maintaining two files and checking both?

When I asked, I was told that they had to do it this way because the people at the message center weren't authorized to update the routing file. That was the responsibility of another agency. So a policy that was established for a paper system where it made sense, was mindlessly applied to a computer system where it did not.

(I pointed out that they apparently were authorized to update the exceptions file. So why not take the official file, carefully label it and put it on a shelf, and then put all the data in the exceptions file and run with that? I don't know if they ever followed up on that suggestion – I moved on to another project.)

In practice, some processes should be directly automated while others should be re-engineered. The trick is to figure out which manual processes transfer well to a computer and which do not.

Users often do not consider re-engineering. They may assume that the database system will be exactly like the manual system, except that it is on a computer. They expect screens to look exactly like their old paper forms. They expect all procedures to be exactly the same. Etc.

The problem with this is: If the computer system will be exactly like the manual system, why bother? If there is absolutely nothing we can do to improve the process, why waste our time and money?

If your users have this attitude, your job is to identify places where re-engineering will be beneficial, and to explain them to the user. Often you will find yourself in the position of trying to convince the user to accept something that will make their lives easier, while they insist on continuing to do it the hard way.

The opposite problem is the user who expects the computer to be a magic box. They think that once the job is transferred to a computer, everything will just happen by itself.

I understood this problem when I started in this business back in the 1970's. Most people back then had never seen a computer outside of a science fiction movie, so they had no idea what these strange machines really could or could not do. I thought that as computers started showing up on people's desks and in their homes, that they would get a more realistic understanding. But apparently not. Many users still expect computers to work like they do on TV: They expect to say, "Computer, give me a list of all the customers who won't pay next month's bill on time," and somehow the computer will do this.

The computer can, of course, do arithmetic and sort lists and manipulate data in all sorts of ways at incredible speeds. But it cannot create information out of thin air. It can only work with what you give it. A computer is not creative. While there have been some limited successes in artificial intelligence, we are a long way from computers that can think out how to solve a problem for themselves: They must be given step by step instructions.

These are often surprisingly difficult concepts for users. Getting past them requires logic and patience.

11.5.   Entity/Attribute Scrubbing

The next step is to try to get a list of entities and attributes.

My general approach has been to explain the concept of entities and attributes to the users, and ask them to list candidates. Explain to them that any blank on any paper form is a candidate attribute. Ask them what "things" these blanks describe.

The users should be able to give you useful information. But don't expect their lists to be correct. They are raw material, not the finished products.

Take their information and go through a process known as "scrubbing". This is cleaning up the information to produce the real list of entities and attributes.

We discussed some of the problems in identifying the correct entities and attributes in chapters 6 and 8. You will have to go through this process with your users, or by yourself after you've finished speaking with the users.

Perhaps the most common problem users have in this area is placing attributes with the correct entity. For example, one day a user might tell you that Tax ID is an attribute of the Office entity. You carefully write this down and move on, until later he gives an example of an office with multiple Tax IDs. Oh, you say, so Tax ID must really be an attribute of some lower-level entity. Department, perhaps? No, he insists, it is an attribute of Office because the office manager must fill out the paperwork to request a Tax ID. You try to explain that we are not asking who applies for it but who it applies to. You will often find that users have a great deal of difficulty comprehending such distinctions. Sometimes they can be resolved by asking simple, clear questions. Like, "So is there a separate Tax ID for each department? Or do all departments in an office have the same ID?" You may need to explain that the question is not who fills out the paperwork or what form it appears on, but who it describes.

Another common problem is that users will confuse the idea of an "entity instance" with an "entity", or an "attribute value" with an "attribute". For example, a user may think that "toaster" is an entity, when it is much more likely that "toaster" is an instance of the Product entity. A user may think that "120 volts" is an attribute, when it is much more likely that the attribute is "Voltage" and one of the possible values is "120". You will then have to explain the difference between a class of things and a specific example of that class, etc.

11.6.   Special Cases

Users often have difficulty identifying all the possible cases that must be considered. When we are designing a database or writing a program, we often come across places where we say, Ah, this thing will be either A or B. The user has told me what to do about A. Now what do I do about B? I can't count the number of times that a user has told me, "Don't worry about that, it almost never happens." I often find myself dealing with admittedly oddball cases, like, What happens if a customer bought something with a credit card, returned it, then used the return value plus some added cash to buy a more expensive model, and now is returning that? Do we give him a cash refund, a credit on his card, or what? I have had a number of occasions when users have gotten visibly angry at me for wasting their time insisting on getting answers about all these unlikely hypothetical cases.

This can be a reasonable position to take with a manual system. We don't bother to give the clerks instructions for every possible oddball situation because most of them will never have to deal with any given odd case. When they do, they ask their supervisor, and half the time he probably makes something up that seems reasonable at the moment.

But we can't tell the computer, "… and if something else comes up, use your judgment." We have to give it specific instructions. Computerizing a previously manual system often results in identifying all sorts of special cases that no one even thought of before.

11.7.   Data versus Processing

Database design is all about determining what data we need to have in our system and how it should be organized. So, do we need to know and understand how this data will be used in order to create a good database design? That is, do we need to know what programs will be written to use this data?

In theory, one might say that the answer is "no". A database design is independent of programming. As long as we know exactly what data is needed, we don't need to know or care how it will be used. A database is supposed to be a model of a real-world subject. What we want to do with that data has nothing to do with what the model looks like. If somehow asks, "How is your company organized?" or "Who approves accounting changes?", I shouldn't need to ask, "Why do you want to know?" before giving an answer. (Unless the questioner is from the government, of course.) Indeed, the theoretician could well argue that there is no way we can know today how the data will be used in the future.

But in practice, that "as long as we know exactly what data is needed" is a huge qualifier. How do we know what data is needed if we don't know what it will be used for?

It often happens in software design that the users say they want the computer system to be able to answer some question, when they have not provided the information necessary to answer it. For example, on one project the users said that they wanted the system to tell them which shipments had not yet been received by the customer. But they shipped products by parcel post: the customer didn't sign for receipt. There was no "receipt date" or "receipt acknowledgement" in the system.

The key question to ask is, "How will the computer know?" If there is no data in the system to satisfy a requirement, then either we need to add attributes for that data – and make sure we have a way to populate the data – or we have to declare the requirement impossible to meet.

11.8. Requirements Creep

There is a regular conflict between the computer people and the users over "requirements creep".

On the one hand, the computer people want the user to tell them up front exactly what they want the system to do and sign a piece of paper saying this is it.

The users want to continually change the requirements as the project goes on.

Both sides have valid positions. For the computer people, it's very difficult to build a database when the users keep changing their minds about what should be in it. We have to have a target to aim at.

But from the users' point of view, we are designing a new product, something that has never existed before. Often the users have little experience with comparable products. They simply don't know how this is all going to fit together until they see it. I'm writing this book for database designers, so let me take the users' side for the moment. Suppose you went out to buy some product, a car say, and instead of showing you various models of car and letting you sit in them and take them for test drives, the dealer took you in a room, handed you a sheet of paper, and demanded that you write down exactly what you wanted in a car. Then he told you that he would find a car meeting that description and he expected you to sign a contract committing to pay for it. Would you agree? Surely you would say, "Wait a minute, I can't describe every single feature that a car could possibly have. I'm not an automotive engineer; I don't necessarily know all the implications of everything I might ask for. I'd have to see it and try it out, and then maybe I'd have to revise my requirements." And you've seen and driven cars before. The user may not have ever seen a database anything like what we are building.

Realistically, then, the requirements process must involve some give and take. The user has to understand that there they cannot change things at any time, at least not without impacting cost and schedule. The database designers have to understand that there must be some flexibility to adjust the requirements as the project proceeds and the users see how this is turning out.

 ## Adventures in Real Life!

A few weeks after deploying version one of a new system, we had a meeting with the big boss of the users to discuss progress in getting users switched from the old system to the new system. At this meeting he described a report he wanted that would help identify left-over problems with bad data from the old system.

I explained that I was sorry, but there was no such report in the system. No such report had ever been mentioned in the requirements, so we had no reason to code for it.

He replied, "I didn't think I needed to put that in the requirements. I just took it for granted that the system would produce any report I needed at any time."

He was completely serious.

11.9. Documentation

I hate paperwork as much as anyone. But there are two documents you should produce for any database project.

The second is the ERD, which we've been discussing for several chapters.

The first is the requirements paper. Get the users to tell you what the requirements are, write it all down, and get them to read it and confirm that this is what they want. It is very easy to misunderstand what someone said in a conversation, or to get confused when ten different users explained something in different words. Often different users have different ideas of what the details of the system operation should be. Furthermore, writing things down helps to focus the mind. Sometimes we think we understand something until we try to explain it to someone else, when suddenly we see the gaps in our knowledge.

By putting all the requirements into one clearly-written document and getting the users to review it and approve it, many misunderstandings, contradictions, and mistakes can be resolved before we spend a lot of time building the wrong system.

This also gives us ammunition if the users try to come back later and change the requirements. We can wave the paper in the air and shout, "Look, this is what you agreed to in August! Here's your signature right here!" Or more realistically, it at least lets us identify when and where the requirements are being changed.

11.10. Coping

You will have to judge your users. If they are very unsophisticated about computers and databases and they are willing to rely on your judgment, you can take what they ask for, go back to your office and turn it into something that makes sense, and then build it.

If your users are reasonably sophisticated or fast learners and they insist on controlling the project, you can explain database design issues to them until they understand them and can give you realistic answers.

The big problem is when the users are unable to understand database design issues, and also demand to control the project. This can and frequently does lead to situations where the users force a bad solution on the database designers, and then blames them for the resultant inevitable failure. There are no easy solutions to this problem. Experts generally give four suggestions: (a) Patiently educate the user on how databases work so that they can make good decisions. (b) Convince the users to trust you and let you make the critical decisions. (c) Document everything so that when it all blows up, you can show them the memo they signed saying this is how it must be done. That is, force the user to take the responsibility for their decisions. (d) Look for another job.

(d) is a good solution if another job is available, but a bit of a cop-out. (c) is basically a strategy of protecting yourself by making sure you can blame someone else. This may be a good fallback, especially if the project gets highly politically charged, but it doesn't sound like a plan conducive to good long-term working relationships. (a) and (b) are positive and productive, but ultimately depends on factors beyond your control. Good luck.

11.11. Review Questions

1. What is the difference between "automation" and "re-engineering"?

2. Why might it be good to know what programs will be written to run against our database when we are designing a database?

3. What is "requirements creep"? What are some methods for controlling it?

12. PHYSICAL MODEL

The only antidote to mental suffering is physical pain.

-- Karl Marx

12.1. Introduction

Building a physical model from a logical model is a fairly straight-forward, mechanical process. Almost.

A logical model is an ideal representation of our data, what we need or what we want it to look like. In order to turn our logical model into something we can actually implement on a real live database product, we have to make a few adjustments. I don't know a generally accepted term for this process, so in this book I will call it "realizing" the model, that is, making it "real".

12.2. Realize the Entities and Attributes

Every entity becomes a "table". Every attribute becomes a "column" in the corresponding table.

This is more a matter of renaming things than actually doing anything.

12.3. Realize the 1:M Relationships

We do this by "posting" a "foreign key" into the "many" side of the relationship. That is, we add columns to the "many" table to hold the primary key of the "one" table.

Example 1: We have a 1:M relationship between Department and Employee. The primary key of Department is "Department ID". So we add a Department ID column to the Employee table

Note that we have to post the "one" into the "many". If we post the Department ID into the Employee table, this is straightforward because there is only one ID to post per employee. If we tried to post the Employee Number into the Department table, we'd have many employees per department, so we'd have to put many employee numbers in each Department record. But how many? Better to do it the easy way. (See section 13.2, First Normal Form.)

Example 2: We have a 1:M relationship between Class Assignment and Test Score. The primary key of Class Assignment is the combination of Class Number and Student Number. To realize the relationship we add both Class Number and Student Number to the Test Score table. That is, a posted foreign key may be a single column or it may be multiple columns.

Sometimes the foreign key is already a column in the table. A common example is when you use it as an identifier of the "many" side of the relationship. In Example 2 above, a likely key for Test Score is Class Number, Student Number, and Test Number. In that case, fine, no need to add a second one or otherwise get complicated. (If you already added the foreign key because you knew you needed it to realize the relationship, that's fine too – you're just running ahead.)

12.4. Realize the 1:1 Relationships

Like for 1:M relationships, we realize the relationship by posting a foreign key.

But which side? This is mostly an arbitrary choice.

If we know that we will routinely find a record in A first and want to find a B from there, rather than the other way around, then it makes sense to post the key of B into A.

If one side is obligatory and the other not, then we may want to post the foreign key in the obligatory side. That way we won't have empty keys on the non-obligatory side.

Besides that, it doesn't make much difference.

12.5.   Realize the M:M Relationships

If there is a M:M relationship between A and B, we can't post the key of A into B, because there could be many of them, and we can't post the key of B into A, for the same reason.

So instead we create a new table to contain the keys of each pair of related records from the original entities.

Example: There is a M:M relationship between Student and Class. The primary key of Student is Student Number; the primary key of Class is Class Number. Clearly this is a many-to-many relationship because each student can take many classes and each class can have many students. We create a new table, Student-Class, to hold this relationship. The data might look like this:

Student Number	Student Name
1001	Fred Miller
1002	Mary Jones
1003	Carl Brun

Class Number	Class Title
CS 101	Java
HI 204	Ancient Rome
SC 309	Hyperdimensional Theory

Class Number	Student Number
CS 101	1001
CS 101	1002
HI 204	1001
HI 204	1003
SC 309	1001
SC 309	1002
SC 309	1003

12.6. Realize Special Relationships

Back in chapters 7 and 8 we discussed two kinds of questionable relationships: relationships that connect more than two entities and relationships that have attributes.

We must create a table for each such special relationship, much as we did for M:M relationships. The procedure is exactly the same.

For relationships with attributes, we include these as columns in the table we create.

For multi-entity relationships, we use the same techniques as discussed in section 7.5 to break the relationship into several relationships each of which connects only two entities/tables.

12.7. Realize Data Types

12.7.1. General

Determine data types for all of our attributes/columns. Classify every column as numeric, character, date, Boolean, or a specialized data type. Determine maximum length. For numbers, is it an integer or can it have decimal places? If it has decimals, is the number of decimal places fixed or is this floating point? Determine any formatting rules, like social security numbers must have hyphens at certain positions. For any codes, find the list of possible values. (This would also be a good time to document what the values mean, though that is not strictly a "database design" task.)

12.7.2. Character types

In SQL, there are three types of character column. "char" is fixed length while "varchar" is variable length. You should usually use char only for short codes – one or two characters -- that have a fixed size.

For longer character strings, the size is usually variable in practice, and assigning to a fixed length column wastes disk space storing spaces. Sometimes longer character strings have a fixed length: a social security number or telephone number, for example. But this fact is rarely useful. In some SQL engines, extra spaces will prevent two character strings from comparing as equal. That is, "Hello " (with a space at the end) is not equal to "Hello" (no space). Other SQL engines will consider them to be equal. For short columns char saves a small amount of space because there's no need to record the length. Sometimes the fact that it can never have zero length is helpful: We don't have to worry about checking for blank, i.e. a single space, *and* empty string, i.e. no characters at all. It is sometimes helpful to be confident that a column is a fixed size when lining up text on a display or print-out.

For truly long character columns, most SQL engines include a "text" or "character large object block (CLOB)" data type. These should be used when a column can contain hundreds or thousands of characters. The data is stored separately from the main record, so this can improve performance on queries that don't refer to the large column. XBase has the "memo" data type, which is the same idea.

12.7.3. Numeric types

Numbers also come in three flavors: integer, fixed decimal, and float. SQL, XBase, and most other database products support these three types. In SQL they are called, respectively, integer, decimal, and float.

When a column can only contain integers of reasonable size, use the integer data type. By "reasonable size" here I mean that you are sure that any input will fit in the computer's integer data type. This usually allows for numbers from about -2 billion to +2 billion, though you should check the documentation of your database product to be sure. This should be plenty big for most quantities that you are likely to encounter in a business database.

Fixed decimal and float are used when you have digits after the decimal point. Fixed, as the name implies, has a fixed number of decimal places, whereas float adjusts the number of decimal places depending on the size of the number.

The advantage of floats is that they can store an extremely broad range of numbers: They typically can hold numbers up to 10^{308}, which is far beyond the range of what we have conventional names for. No matter the scale they hold the same number of significant digits, about 15. The drawback to floats is that the number is not exact. You can set a float equal to, say, .1234567, and when you retrieve it, it is now .1234568. This is because floats are stored in binary, not decimal, and the translation between binary and decimal fractions is not always exact.

Fixed point numbers, on the other hand, have a much narrower range, but are exact.

Thus, floats are most often used for measurements, like temperature or volume, where having a wide range and many digits after the decimal is desirable, but the last digit isn't necessarily meaningful. There is, after all, no such thing as an "exact measurement". A measurement is only as accurate as the instruments used to make it.

Use fixed for amounts of money, where we definitely do not want to enter "$32.17" and get back "$32.1699".

Fixed point can also be used for numbers too big to fit in an integer, as it usually allows more positions.

In general, integers take the least space and can be processed most quickly. Floats are next. Fixed point is biggest and slowest.

12.7.4. Date types

The date types are more straightforward. If you need to store just a date, use date. If you need to store a time, use time. If you need to store a date and time, use timestamp.

About the only tricky thing here is that you have to be careful when comparing dates to timestamps. The behavior varies depending on the database product. In Oracle and mySQL, when you compare a date to a timestamp it behaves as if the date had a time of midnight. That is, date '1986-12-10' < timestamp '1986-12-10 08:30:00'. Postgres ignores the time portion of the timestamp in comparisons, so date '1986-12-10'=timestamp '1986-12-10 08:30:00'.

12.7.5. Consistency

Make sure that any column that occurs in more than one table has the identical data type and size everywhere it is found. I am not saying you should violate the rules against redundancy here. See section 8.4. For example, the foreign keys of a child record must match the data type of the primary key of the parent record. Many annoying problems have been caused by a primary key that was a sequence number with a maximum length of six digits, but the database designer used a foreign key defined as only five digits, and everything works fine until record number 100,000 is created.

12.8. Add Lookup Tables

We often have attributes that have a finite set of possible values. For example, we may have an "Account Type" that can be checking, savings, money market, CD, or investment; or an "Order Status" that can be in-process, held, shipped, or received. We want the system to know the valid values and not allow others in. But we don't want to hard-code this in our programs because the list of values may change over time.

A common solution is to create lookup tables with lists of all the legal values of such codes. Typically a lookup table has just two columns: an id to use as a key, and a name or description. Sometimes there's only one: A code that serves as both the key and the name. It is debatable whether these qualify as entities because they do not really meet the requirement that we "keep information about them". All we're keeping is the fact of their existence. But in practice it is very helpful to have the list. So we do not normally list them as entities in the logical model, but when we realize the physical model, we add them in. (Also, lookup tables can really clutter up an otherwise elegant Entity-Relationship Diagram.)

If you have a lookup table with more information than this, it is not a lookup table but a true entity. Example: You are tempted to call "State" (as in Alabama or New York) a lookup table. The table contains two columns: state abbreviation and name. This is a lookup table. But if you say, "and sales tax rate", it is now an entity. You are keeping actual data about it.

If you do not have a complete list of the code values by now, this would be a good time to collect it.

12.9. Making and Splitting 1:1s

Sometimes it is desirable for efficiency reasons to break the columns of a table across two smaller tables. That is, put some of the columns in one table and some in another, and then create a 1:1 relationship between them.

There are basically two reasons to do this:

One, if there are some columns in a table that are often blank or null, dragging these empty columns around can hurt performance. So instead we can break these columns off into an "auxiliary table", and only join on it when we need it.

For example, our museum collection management system has an entity for Accession that includes many different kinds of exhibits that we might display in our museum. To support paintings, we include attributes for name of the artist, date painted, name of the model, artistic style, and so on. These attributes do not apply to exhibits in the natural history section or the technology section. Thus, it might be a good idea to break these out into a separate table.

However, most database engines today compress blank columns down to little or no space. This is much less of an issue than it was at one time. Still, it takes the database engine *some* time to skip over unneeded columns.

Breaking up a table with many columns can also make it more manageable for human beings reading the schema. If the division is logical – if after the break-up each table contains columns that logically go together – this might make it easier to understand. (If the division is truly logical, we should have split them in the logical model.)

Two and more important, if there are some columns that are rarely used, and especially if these columns are large, this can be an extra load to carry around. A database engine must normally read an entire record at a time, so if most of the data is irrelevant most of the time, including it all in one table can mean a lot of wasted effort.

Suppose our Accession table includes columns for Category, Display Room Number and Insured Value that are used all the time, and also a column for Description that is a free-form text field that is only used when we are updating the plaques that we place on the display cases once every few years. Category, Display Room Number, and Insured Value are likely short fields, just a few characters each. Description is likely quite long. It is quite possible that 90% of the disk space taken up by this table is the Description. So when we are running routine reports, in order to get the five or ten digits of insured value for each record we have to also read hundreds of characters of description. This can really slow down queries. It makes sense to break the Description out into a separate table with a 1:1 relationship to the main table. This is especially true if you have several large such columns, or many smaller columns whose sizes add up.

Many modern database engines have special data types for large text columns that store this data separately without the need for you to create separate tables. In effect, they create separate tables for you invisibly. Some SQL dialects have "character large object blocks" (CLOBs) or "text" data types that work like this, and XBase has the "memo" data type. In that case, just relax and let the engine do the work for you.

There are also times when you might want to do the reverse: take two tables that have a 1:1 relationship and combine them into a single table. If both tables have few columns, or if you expect that any time one is used you will be joining it with the other, it could be smart to combine them. If the relationship is obligatory on both ends the argument for this is quite strong.

Note this discussion is in some ways similar to the discussion we had in section 7.2.3. The difference is that there we discussing when two entities should *logically* be a single entity or vice versa, while here we are discussing when there are *physical*, i.e. efficiency, reasons to split or combine.

Some experts would say that these decisions should be deferred to implementation time, see chapter 15.

12.10. Review Questions

1. What do we mean by "realizing" a model?

2. Name two database objects that are realized as tables.

3. How do we realize a one-to-many relationship?

4. How do we realize a one-to-one relationship?

5. How do we realize a many-to-many relationship?

6. What special kinds of relationships require us to create additional tables?

13. NORMALIZATION

Nothing is poetical if plain daylight is not poetical; and no monster should amaze us if the normal man does not amaze.

-- G. K. Chesterton

13.1. Introduction

"Normalization" refers to certain ways of structuring a database to avoid redundancy and unnecessary complexity. Normalization was invented and named by Edgar F. Codd, a British computer scientist who worked for IBM in the 1970s.

The usual way of describing normalization is to start out with a database design that has many problems and then clean it up by progressing through a series of "normal forms". These are called simply "first normal form", "second normal form", and "third normal form", and are abbreviated "1N", "2N", and "3N". Since Codd, other theorists have added 4N and 5N.

In real life, we normally (no pun intended) normalize our database design *before* we realize the physical model. But normalization is difficult to describe or understand without reference to foreign keys, which don't come up until we get to the physical model, and normalization is typically discussed using physical model terms like "table", so I'm putting this chapter out of chronological order.

13.2. First Normal Form

To be in First Normal Form, or 1N, a table must (a) Have a primary key; and (b) Have no repeating groups.

We discussed primary keys in chapter 9.

By no repeating groups, I mean that you cannot have more than one column with the same definition. To put it another way, any multi-valued fact must have a separate record for each value. A "multi-valued fact" means an attribute or column that can occur more than once for a given key value. A one-to-many relationship is an example of a multi-valued fact, but we could have a multi-valued fact without the "multi" part connecting to another entity: it could be a simple attribute.

Example: A system for an insurance company lists family members covered by a policy. There could be many family members under a single policy, so this is a multi-valued fact. For each family member we must keep the name, sex, and birth date. The Policy table has columns for Policy Number, Plan Type, perhaps other columns that describe the type of policy, deductibles, whatever, and then: Name-1, Sex-1, Birthdate-1, Name-2, Sex-2, Birthdate-2, Name-3, Sex-3, Birthdate-3, etc, for as many family members as we provide for.

This is a violation of the "no repeating groups rule". A strong clue that you are breaking this rule is when column names include a number.

Such a table can be brought up to 1N by breaking the list of family members out into a separate table. That is, we remove all the family members from the Policy table. Then we create a new Family Member table, with one record for each family member on the policy, and with a many-to-one relationship to Policy.

That is, the unnormalized way to do it is:

```
Policy (policy number*, plan type^, name-1,
sex-1, birthdate-1, name-2, sex-2, birthdate-2,
name-3, sex-3, birthdate-3, name-4, sex-4,
birthdate-4)
```

In real life we would probably need to keep more information about each family member than this, and we would surely have to allow for more than four family members, but you get the idea. A more realistic example would be even more tedious.

Data might look like this. (Note that unlike all the other tables in this book, I put this one with rows and columns switched because there are otherwise too many columns to fit on the page. This is a symptom of the lack of normalization.)

Policy Number	10247	13579
Plan Type	C	A
Name 1	Bradley Dover	Robert Smith
Sex 1	M	M
Birthdate 1	08/03/1972	03/12/1961
Name 2	Li Dover	Belinda Smith
Sex 2	F	F
Birthdate 2	10/30/1971	06/15/1964
Name 3	Amy Dover	Ehud Smith
Sex 3	F	M
Birthdate 3	12/02/2001	09/14/1996
Name 4		Jael Smith
Sex 4		F
Birthdate 4		04/28/1999

The first-normal way is:

```
Policy (policy number*, plan type^)
Family Member (family member id*, policy
number^, name, sex, birthdate)
```

Policy Number	Plan Type
10247	C
13579	A

Family Member ID	Policy Number	Name	Sex	Birthdate
239871	10247	Bradley Dover	M	08/03/1972
239872	10247	Li Dover	F	10/30/1971
259374	10247	Amy Dover	F	12/02/2001
327041	13579	Robert Smith	M	03/12/1961
327102	13579	Belinda Smith	F	06/15/1964
329046	13579	Ehud Smith	M	09/14/1996
331098	13579	Jael Smith	F	04/28/1999

Why is this better?

First, just looking at the unnormalized and normalized examples should show that the normalized example is easier to read. Someone creating or updating the tables might easily miss one of the columns in those long repetitive lists. If there is some variation – like maybe there are really two different kinds of family members, some who have an additional column and some who don't – it would be easy for someone reading the list to miss that fact. And someone reading the list who did realize that there might be variations would be forced to study the list to make sure there are not.

Second, we eliminate the problem of having to know the maximum in advance and allow for it. What is the most children a family could possibly have? That's very hard to say. Systems like this often run into trouble because somebody said "we'll allow for ten – I can't imagine anyone having more than ten children". Then the next day a family with 12 kids signs up and the system fails. In the normalized version, this is not a problem: We create as many Family Member records as we need, until we run out of disk space.

Third, how do we know how many there are? We can add a "count" column, but then that's one more column we have to process and keep current. What happens if the count is three but in fact four entries are filled in? What does this mean? Some designers rely on blanks or nulls or some other special value to mean "not used". In this case a blank name might mean that this is an unused entry, because everyone should have a name. Right? Maybe not. It is likely that our insurance covers new-born babies. What if someone submits a claim for care of their newborn in the hospital nursery before they've decided on a name? With the normalized version, the problem evaporates. There is one record in the Family Member table for each family member. There's no need or reason to create dummy records to fill out some arbitrary maximum.

Fourth, we simplify processing. With the unnormalized version, when we want to read the family members, we must loop through the occurrences within a record, stopping when we get to an empty one. Or perhaps we have to skip empty ones. Do we allow for 1, 2, and 4 to be filled while 3 is empty? When we delete an entry – say a child grows up and is no longer covered under mom's or dad's insurance – can we just blank out his entry or do we have to slide all the higher entries down to fill in the space? When we add an entry, we have to search for an available slot. Etc. None of this is mind-numbingly difficult to do, of course, but it's extra work that we don't need. In the normalized version, all of this goes away. When we add a new family member, we create a new Family Member record. When we remove a family member, we delete a Family Member record. Then we let the database engine worry about managing space.

Most important, this normalization dramatically simplifies our queries. Suppose we want to find the family member named "Sally Smith". With the unnormalized database, we would have to write "where name1='Sally Smith' or name2='Sally Smith' or name3='Sally Smith' or name4='Sally Smith'". If later we discover the limit was not large enough and we have to add another slot, we have to remember to modify all the queries to check this new slot. With the normalized database, there's only one name to check.

When we get to a real implementation, there are also storage and performance considerations. As we must allow for the maximum, it follows that in most cases, most of the columns will be blank, which may mean a lot of wasted space on disk. (Most modern databases have methods for compressing blank space, but it still costs us something.) Instead of having a single index on, say, "name", we will need a separate index for each of the name columns. Etc.

Yes, we had to create an additional table, which may be a pain. But the price is well worth the benefit.

As always, there are hazy cases. What if we have more than one of something, but they're not interchangeable? In this example, while the policy holder is presumably also a family member, it is likely that we need to distinguish the policy holder from other family members.

There are three ways to deal with this. (a) Say that they are not really a repeating group: they are really different columns that happen to share a domain. (b) Create an additional column in the child table to identify the "type". In the insurance example, we might create an additional column in the Family Member table for "policy holder", which would be true for the policy holder and false for all other family members. (c) Create an additional column in the parent table that holds the key of the "special" child record.

(c) is generally discouraged as it brings its own problems. It quickly gets out of hand if there is more than one special record, because we then need multiple "special" columns. Also, it introduces the potential problem that the record we're pointing to may not point back, and so we have inconsistent pointers.

 ## Adventures in Real Life!

In a system for managing technical manuals, each manual had an "administrative manager", who was responsible for arranging to get it printed, deciding who in the organization needed copies, and that sort of thing. There was also a "stock manager", who was responsible for keeping track of the inventory and responding to requests for copies. And there was a "technical content manager", who actually wrote the book. Often two or even all three of these jobs would be done by the same person, and each person was usually responsible for many manuals.

So for this part of the requirements I created two tables: Person held things like Name and Department and Email Address, and included records for all types of "managers". (As well as other people of interest to our system, but that's not relevant here.) Technical Manual included Manual Number, Title, Publication Date, and lots of other columns, including three columns for Administrative Manager, Stock Manager, and Technical Content Manager.

Big mistake. By creating three separate columns, I multiplied my headaches by three. There were many places in

---

the system that cared about the managers, and most of them had to do their work three times.

A common thing for a manager to want to know is, "What books am I responsible for?" or some information about those books. Every one of these queries had to check all three columns. We had to provide for the possibility of someone quitting and being replaced. Again, we would have to check all three columns. Etc etc.

If I'd created a separate table, there would have been only one column to check in all these cases.

Yes, sometimes we only cared about one of the types of manager. But that would have been easy enough: include a column in the Manager table for "manager type", with three possible values. Then when we're only interested in, say, technical content managers, we add "and manager_type='TCM'" to our query. When we don't care which kind of manager, we don't mention it.

My rule of thumb: If two columns are really used in completely different contexts even though they share a domain, it is legitimate to preserve them as two columns. For example, "date of birth" and "date hired" are both dates and so will resemble each other, but it's hard to imagine someone asking, "Tell me all the employees either born in 1982 or hired in 1982". But if the two are even somewhat interchangeable, break them out into a separate table. When in doubt, break them out into a separate table.

13.3. Second Normal Form

To be in second normal form, or 2N, there must be no "partial dependencies". That is, there must not be any columns in the table that are dependent on some, but not all, columns of any multi-column key.

For example, suppose we have a class registration database. We create a table like this:

Class (class number*, class title, instructor, student number*, student name, grade)

Data might look like:

Class number	Class title	Instructor	Student Number	Student Name	Grade
CS 101	Java	Smith	1032	Burman	A
CS 101	Java	Smith	1243	Chavelle	B
CS 101	Java	Smith	1492	Columbus	B
CS 102	C++	Miller	1066	Norman	C
CS 102	C++	Miller	1243	Chavelle	D
CS 204	Data Structures	Corwin	1032	Burman	A
CS 204	Data Structures	Corwin	1243	Chavelle	B
CS 204	Data Structures	Corwin	2217	Chang	A

The key is Class Number plus Student Number. Neither alone is enough to uniquely identify a record.

This table fails Second Normal Form because there are several columns that depend on only one of the two columns that make up the key. Class Title and Instructor depend only on Class Number. The class does not have a different name and a different teacher for each student, so they do not depend on Student Number. Likewise Student Name depends only on Student Number. Students do not change their names when they attend different classes. Indeed in this example, the only column that *does* depend on the full key is Grade.

To achieve 2N, we break this table into three separate tables:

Class (class number*, class title, instructor)
Student (student number*, student name)
Registration (class number*, student number*, grade)

Our data would then look like this:

Class Number	Class Title	Instructor
CS 101	Java	Smith
CS 102	C++	Miller
CS 204	Data Structures	Corwin

Student Number	Student Name
1032	Burman
1066	Norman
1243	Chavelle
1492	Columbus
2217	Chang

Class Number	Student Number	Grade
CS 101	1032	A
CS 101	1243	B
CS 101	1492	B
CS 102	1066	C
CS 102	1243	D
CS 204	1032	A
CS 204	1243	B
CS 204	2217	A

Why is this better?

It eliminates redundancy. In Figure 8.1, the Class Title, Instructor Name, and Student Name are repeated over and over. Not only is this wasteful, but it creates three "anomalies": The update anomaly, the delete anomaly, and the insert anomaly.

The update anomaly: Recall back in section 8.4 we discussed the problems of redundant data. Those same problems apply here. In Normalization terminology, consistency problems are called the "update anomaly". Suppose in the above example we updated the CS 101 / student 1032 record to change the class title to "Krakatoa". Now one record says that CS 101 is "Krakatoa" while two others say that it is "Java". Which is it?

The delete anomaly: Suppose all the students in CS 102 drop the class, so we delete their records. But now we have lost all information about CS 102. The class has apparently been dropped from our course catalog. We can never teach it again. If all the students in a class drop out, maybe we should be canceling the course forever, but we don't want our database to decide that for us. That should be up to the department chairman.

The insert anomaly: Suppose we create a new class. We don't yet have any students. How do we add a class to the course catalog with no students? Perhaps we could fill in blanks or nulls for the student related information. But then when we get our first student, do we delete the record with the blanks? A seemingly simple operation like "count how many students are in a class" suddenly becomes complicated: we have to watch our for "dummy student" records. Some database engines do not allow null values in keys, so this might not even be possible. Yes, if our database has such a rule, we could always make up a fake student number, like "9999". But then we have to be careful not to assign this fake student number to any real student, and we have to be continually checking for it.

Note that a table fails 2N if there are columns that depend on part of *any* key, not just the primary key. Developers sometimes think they have achieved 2N by creating a new key with a single column. Then they say that everything in the table is dependent on the full key, i.e. the single column. Sorry, no, there is no such loophole in the rules. Creating a new key does not make the old key go away.

If all keys have only one column (one column each, that is), then the 2N test is simple. If there is only one column in the key, then we can't have part of the key, because you can't have less than one column. So if all keys – or the only key – have only one column, there's no need to work very hard to determine whether you meet 2N. You do.

While it is not obvious in a textbook problem, 2N can save a lot of resources. When we achieve 2N, we remove redundant columns from a table and move one copy of them into a separate table. In the example above, we have two or three students for each class. So normalizing the table means we eliminated one or two copies of the class information, at the price of creating a new table. Big deal. But in a real database, there probably aren't just two or three students for each class. Over the course of several years we could build up a database of hundreds or thousands. So we're really talking about removing several hundred copies of each class title and instructor name. Furthermore, in a real database, there are probably a lot more than two columns of class data. The savings in disk space, and the time required to read all this data from disk, are significant.

13.4. Third Normal Form

To be in third normal form, we must have no "transitive dependencies". That is, there may not be any columns that depend on something other than the key.

Example: We have a personnel system that includes an Employee table, like this:

Employee (employee number*, name, hire date, department id, department name, department manager)

The data might be something like this:

Employee Number	Name	Hire Date	Dept ID	Dept Name	Dept Manager
1001	Bob Smith	Mar 7, 2007	AC	Accounting	Fred Stover
1002	Mary Lewis	Aug 16, 2006	AC	Accounting	Fred Stover
1003	Kevin Petrowski	Dec 9, 1994	EN	Engineering	Bryan Callahan
1004	Allen Dukas	Feb 20, 1995	EN	Engineering	Bryan Callahan
1005	Jennifer Suko	Oct 14, 2004	SA	Sales	Karen Dilmer

Perhaps the redundancy is obvious. We need the Department ID on each record to tell us which department the employee works in. But the Department Name and Department Manager are repeated unnecessarily. These depend solely on the Department ID.

To achieve 3N we must split this department information into a separate table:

Employee (employee number*, name, hire date, department id^)
Department (department id*, department name, department manager)

The data would then look like this:

Employee Number	Name	Hire Date	Dept ID
1001	Bob Smith	Mar 7, 2007	AC
1002	Mary Lewis	Aug 16, 2006	AC
1003	Kevin Petrowski	Dec 9, 1994	EN
1004	Allen Dukas	Feb 20, 1995	EN
1005	Jennifer Suko	Oct 14, 2004	SA

Dept ID	Dept Name	Dept Manager
AC	Accounting	Fred Stover
EN	Engineering	Bryan Callahan
SA	Sales	Karen Dilmer

Why is this better?

Pretty much the same answer as for 2N: It eliminates redundancy and avoids the three anomalies.

Some find the difference between 3N and 2N confusing. 2N is "no partial key dependencies". 3N is "no transitive dependencies". That is, 2N says you cannot have any columns dependent on only part of any key. 3N says you cannot have columns dependent on something other than the key. Note that in this example, Department ID is not part of the key. We do not need the Department ID to help identify an employee.

"Transitive" is a mathematical term referring to a chain of relationships, like a<b and b<c implies that a<c. So a "transitive dependency" is when a depends on b and b depends on c, so there is an indirect dependency of a on c. In this case, Department Name and Manager depend on Department ID, and Department ID depends on Employee Number, so Department Name and Manager depend on Employee Number indirectly.

As for 2N, disk space savings can be dramatic.

"I SWEAR THAT EVERY COLUMN DEPENDS ON THE KEY, THE WHOLE KEY AND NOTHING BUT THE KEY, SO HELP ME CODD."

13.5. Fourth Normal Form

To be in fourth normal form, a table may not have two or more independent multi-valued facts.

Suppose our company has a number of Offices. Each office may or may not participate in various employee benefit programs. Some choose to offer the company dental plan; others don't. Some offer the 401k; others don't. Etc. Each Office also has a "territory", a set of states where they are responsible for selling products. What states an Office markets to and what benefits the Office participates in have nothing to do with each other. That is, if an Office sells in both Ohio and Indiana, they won't offer a dental plan when an employee is calling customers in Indiana but not when she is calling customers in Ohio.

These are two multi-valued facts: state and benefit. Suppose we try to put both multi-valued facts in one table. We might get something like this:

Office	State	Benefit
Boston	MA	Dental
Boston	MA	Flextime
Boston	CT	Dental
Boston	CT	Flextime
Dayton	OH	Dental
Dayton	OH	401k
Dayton	IN	Dental
Dayton	IN	401k
Tampa	AL	401k
Tampa	FL	401k
Tampa	GA	401k

To remove the independent multi-valued facts and achieve 4N, we break this into two tables:

Office	State
Boston	CT
Boston	MA
Dayton	OH
Dayton	IN
Tampa	AL
Tampa	FL
Tampa	GA

Office	Benefit
Boston	Dental
Boston	Flextime
Dayton	Dental
Dayton	401k
Tampa	401k

Why is this better?

When both multi-valued facts are in one table, we have redundant data. In this example, the list of benefits must be repeated for every state and the list of states must be repeated for every benefit. This creates the possibility that we could introduce errors into the data by failing to include all the combinations. When it is broken into two tables, this possible error evaporates.

We also have the same insert and delete anomalies that we have seen before. What happens if an office drops all benefit plans? Suddenly all their assigned states disappear. Our employees might not like being expected to make sales without being offered any benefits, but one would think this is not impossible to do.

4N can save huge amounts of disk space. In this textbook problem, that may not be apparent. But suppose we market to all 50 states and we have 5 benefit programs. If we create one record for each state and one record for each benefit program, that's 50 plus 5 equals 55 records. But if we have to create a benefit record for each state, that's 50 *times* 5 equals 250. As the number of combinations grows, the normalized disk space grows as the sum, while the unnormalized disk space grows as the product.

Don't forget that key word *independent*. Suppose each Office is assigned certain Products that it is supposed to sell, but it may be assigned different products in different states. The Boston office may sell toasters in Massachusetts and Connecticut, but it is responsible for blenders only in Massachusetts, and the Richmond office handles blenders in Connecticut. In this case the two multi-value facts are not independent, so it is correct to have a table that ties all three things together. If we tried to separate Office-State and Office-Product into two tables, there would be no way to tell which products apply to any given state. When the two multi-valued facts are dependent, they belong in one table. When they are independent, they belong in separate tables.

13.6.   Fifth Normal Form

To be in fifth normal form, every join dependency must be implied by the candidate keys.

This one is pretty obscure. Frankly, I don't think I've ever worried about this on a real project.

The common type of example given is this: We have many offices, each offering a variety of products. For each product, we have several possible extended service plans: we may warrant the product for 3 years for one price and for 5 years for a higher price. Every office that sells a product must offer all available warranties for that product, but there may be different warranties for different products.

Under these rules, the following table fails 5N:

Office	Product	Service Plan
Dayton	Toaster	3 year
Dayton	Toaster	5 year
Wendover	Blender	1 year
Wendover	Blender	2 year
Charlottesville	Toaster	3 year
Charlottesville	Toaster	5 year
Charlottesville	Blender	1 year
Charlottesville	Blender	2 year

In 4N, we are concerned about two independent multi-value facts in the same table. Here, we are concerned about two *related* multi-value facts in the same table. We can't have Dayton/Toaster/3 without having Dayton/Toaster/5, so by specifying both, we create the possibility that we might have left one out, which is supposed to be impossible.

This schema can be normalized by breaking it into two tables:

Office	Product
Dayton	Toaster
Wendover	Blender
Charlottesville	Toaster
Charlottesville	Blender

Product	Service Plan
Toaster	3 year
Toaster	5 year
Blender	1 year
Blender	2 year

13.7. Summary

Normal Form	Rule
First Normal Form	primary key, no repeating groups
Second Normal Form	no partial dependencies
Third Normal Form	no transitive dependencies
Fourth Normal Form	no independent multi-valued facts
Fifth Normal Form	every join dependency must be implied by the candidate keys

13.8. Review Questions

1. What is First Normal Form?

2. What is a multi-valued fact?

3. How does 1N simplify programming?

4. What is Second Normal Form?

5. What are the "insert anomaly", the "update anomaly", and the "delete anomaly"?

6. What is Third Normal Form?

7. What does the word "transitive", as used here, mean?

8. What is Fourth Normal Form?

9. What is Fifth Normal Form?

10. How does normalization save disk space and access time?

14. Scope

None can love freedom heartily but good men; the rest love not freedom, but license which never hath more scope than under tyrants.

-- John Milton

Students of database design often ask, "How many entities should I have in my model? How many attributes?" Etc.

The correct but non-useful answer is, "It depends. You should have as many as are required to model your data."

A better (but no doubt still unsatisfying) answer is, "More than you think." It is easy to underestimate the size of the model that we will need. When we are first thinking about a problem, we tend to think about it in broad generalizations. It is not until we study the requirements that we discover a maze of annoying little details.

Adventures
in Real Life!

I often participate in on-line forums for programmers and analysts. I've noticed that people will frequently make posts on these forums claiming that they could easily solve some problem that is bedeviling another poster with a week or two of programming.

On one forum recently, a poster described problems he was having with a system to track donations for a non-profit organization. Someone else then posted that he could easily build such a system in a couple of weeks. All you need, he said, is a database with two tables: Donor, to hold name, address, phone number, maybe a few other things; and Donation, with the date, amount of the donation, and credit card number. Then you create a couple of screens to enter the data and you're done.

I wonder if the poster was a student or recent graduate who failed to consider the differences between a class assignment and a real world problem. Such a simple system might be a solution to a classroom exercise, where many difficulties are assumed away. But it is extremely unlikely that it would be useful to a real organization. It doesn't begin to address all the likely complexities.

For starters, are all payments made by credit card? What if the donor wants to pay by cash or check?

Do we give out any little gifts to the donors, like mugs or tote bags? If so, we have to record somewhere which gift a donor selected and whether we've sent it yet.

What reports do we need to get out of the system? Surely someone wants to know how much we've raised, whether some fund-raising drives are more successful than others, and all sorts of other questions. Does this create new data requirements?

Are there government regulations we have to comply with?

Etc, etc.

And any real system I've ever worked on always turns out to have obscure little rules. There's always an exception for accounts opened before 1983 or mileage in California or some such. These special cases can account for 1% of the data and 40% of the design time.

I don't believe that you could identify and document the *requirements* for such a system in less than a month, never mind actually build it.

(Perhaps I should clarify that I do not fault teachers for giving simplified problems as classroom exercises. The point of an exercise is to give the students practice in the subject of the lesson – how to use a SQL create statement or a Java sub-class or whatever. The lesson would be lost if the student got bogged down in analyzing a hundred special cases. The examples in this book are all highly simplified, too. Perhaps computer science teachers should make an effort to make clear to students that real-world problems will not be this simple.)

Consider a very small, easy system I worked on a few years back: A system to track change requests for other computer systems. The basic requirements were straightforward: Users enter a change request into a web page. This request includes some identification of the system they are requesting changes to, a description of the desired change, and various information about the change. These change requests are then be forwarded to a committee for evaluation. Notification emails are sent to interested persons when action is taken on a request.

You might at first think that the database would consist of just two entities: System and Change Request.

But wait. We had to track which user made the request and be able to send him email notifications. So we had to have a User entity to hold the id and email address.

We had to know who to route requests to. That meant there was a Change Request Board entity that held the members of the committee for each system. We defined it to have one record for each board member, with a M:1 relationship to System. It included some information about each member, like which was the chairman and which were voting members and which were non-voting members. As board members were all also system users, rather than repeating user information we had a M:1 relationship between Board and User. (A single User could be on many Boards with different roles.)

Often other users would want to comment on a change request, giving additional ideas about how it should be done, or perhaps disagreeing with the whole idea. So we had to have a Comment entity with a M:1 relationship to Change Request.

Often users wanted to include screen shots showing a problem screen, or diagrams of their proposal, etc. So we provided a way to upload such additional documents and created an Attachment entity to hold references to them.

Board members could vote to approve or disapprove each change request. We had to record the results of this vote. We couldn't store a board member's vote in the Board record, because a given board member could vote on many change requests. And besides, the members of the board changed regularly, the people on the board when a vote was taken might be totally different from the people on the board today. So we created a Vote entity, M:M to User (not Board), and M:M to Change Request.

Then we had to identify what Release a Change would be included in. We needed information about a Release like release number and date. Another entity.

There's probably more that I'm forgetting – it's been years and I don't have access to that system any more. But here a trivially simple system requires at least 8 entities and 13 relationships. See Figure 14.1. Most of these are not obvious at first glance.

I tend to do a lot more entity consolidation (see section 6.2) than most database designers, but I still find that most of my databases for real problems require at least a twenty or thirty entities. It is common to see databases with hundreds or even thousands of entities. Many of these very complex databases are the result of poor design. They often have a lot of redundant data and poorly defined entities. If you have more than one hundred entities, you should study your schema and see if you can't simplify it. But it's certainly not impossible for it to be that big and be the cleanest possible design.

Consider a simple entity like Customer. If you allow more than one address – like a shipping address and a billing address – by the rules of normalization that must be broken into a separate entity. Today people have many phone numbers – home, work, cell – so there's another entity. If you keep credit card or bank draft information, the customer can surely have more than one method of payment, so there's another entity. Etc.

Attributes tend to multiply quickly, too. You might start out saying your Customer entity will have name, address, city, state, zip, and phone number. But you quickly find that you have to add all sorts of status code and dates and what not.

It's a very rare entity that doesn't have at least one relationship. Two or three is probably typical. If your ERD is broken into unconnected pieces, that is, if an insect walking along relationship lines could not get from any entity to any other entity, that's suspicious too. There's nothing inherently wrong with it, but you should investigate.

In short, don't panic if the size of your schema starts to multiply. This is normal. But keep on eye on it.

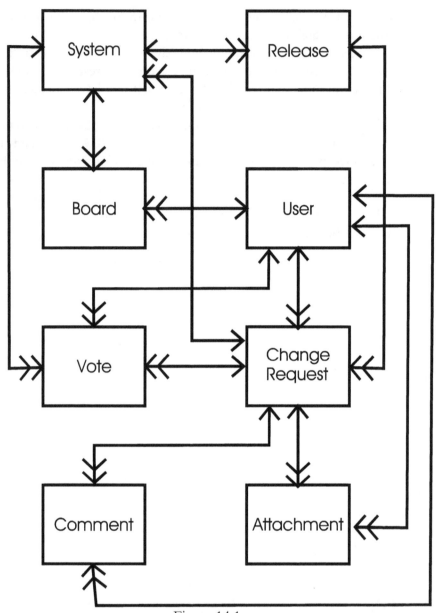

Figure 14.1

15. IMPLEMENTATION

Strategy equals execution. All the great ideas and visions in the world are worthless if they can't be implemented rapidly and efficiently.

-- Colin Powell

15.1. Implementation Day

Finally the day has arrived when we are ready to sit down in front of the computer and start actually creating a real live database. Implementing the model is the process of translating the physical model into a language that can be understood by a commercial database product.

15.2. Freedom and Regimentation

When we're building logical and physical models, we can be very free and loose in how we describe things. When it's all in a word processor or a general-purpose drawing program there are no specific requirements for style and format. We can freely scribble "alpha" or "character" or "text" or whatever strikes our fancy. This is good, because it lets us concentrate on figuring out what the system we're designing is supposed to do and not have to worry about nit-picky details of syntax.

But when we begin to actually implement, the rules become more pedantic. Suddenly little things like a misspelled word or a missing semicolon become crucial. Now we have to be concerned with the details of a real live computer and a real live database language.

15.3. Prematurely Physical

Note that nothing that I have said before this depends on the database language. (Except for chapter 5, of course.) You can do all the work of designing your database, up to and including the physical model, without knowing or caring what database engine you will ultimately use. I have used SQL for examples, but I could just as well have used a different dialect of SQL or a completely different language, like XBase, without changing the idea conveyed.

This is not simply an amusing philosophical point. When designing any computer system, it is important to remember to look at the problem before you decide on a solution. This may sound obvious when stated that way, but users and developers often make assumptions about what the solution must be before they have done any analysis to justify it.

Deciding what database engine we will use, what programming language, or what hardware, before we have analyzed the requirements, is called "getting prematurely physical".

Sometimes assumptions about the solution are brazenly written into requirements documents. I once had an ~~argument~~ conversation with my boss at the time when he insisted that our requirements document should specify what language the programs would be written in, what database product it would use, what server it would run on, and other details about software tools and specific hardware.

These things are not "requirements", but assumptions about the solution.

Adventures
in Real Life!

As a consultant I was given a task of developing a small system interface that required us to upload a file from a web page. One of the "requirements" was that it had to be written in ASP. I pointed out to the customer that ASP has no built-in feature to do file uploads, and I suggested that we write it in PHP instead. The customer insisted that it must be written in ASP. They also prohibited using any open source software, so I had to either search for a commercial product to do file uploads with ASP or write the code myself. What could have been a job requiring several days of work become several weeks.

Different database products have different pros and cons. It makes much more sense to decide on a database product after we know what we are trying to accomplish rather than before. For example, Microsoft Access is cheap and easy to install and works fine for a single user on a single computer. But it was never designed to be used with hundreds of simultaneous users, and if you try, it becomes slow and unreliable. On the other hand, Oracle can handle very large numbers of users and very large databases very well. But it is relatively complicated to install, configure, and keep running smoothly. So Oracle is a good choice for a system that will have a single server shared by hundreds of users. In those circumstances we can afford to have people skilled in Oracle on hand to manage the database. It is a poor choice for a system where each user is expected to install a copy on his own computer. It's like the difference between a pick-up truck and a sports car. Neither is inherently "better" or "worse" without reference to the intended use. If you are planning to haul refrigerators, the pick-up truck is surely better. If you are planning to compete in a race, the sports car is superior.

Of course, there are times when it is a good idea to use a certain database product (or programming language or other tool) even though it is not the best for this particular job. There is something to be said for having all or most of your systems on the same database product. Then the staff can spend their time mastering one product instead of many, we don't have to spend money for multiple similar products, sharing data between systems is easier, and so on. The fact that another product has some feature that would be useful in one small system may not outweigh the disadvantages.

But these should be conscious choices made after we know the facts, and not blind assumptions that we make without even thinking about them.

Of course if you boss tells you, "Our standard here is that all systems will use Oracle because my brother works for Oracle and he has a family to support" ... well then, from the developer's point of view, that may be just as much a requirement as any.

"HEY D.B., LET'S NOT GET PREMATURELY PHYSICAL."

15.4. Database Languages

Most database products on the market today use Structured Query Language, or SQL. Oracle, MySQL, Postgres, and Microsoft SQL Server are examples of SQL-based database products.

DBase and FoxPro use XBase as their "native language", though these have long since added SQL support. There are a scattering of other database products that use proprietary languages.

Many database engines have a front end of some sort that allows you to manipulate the database with pretty, easy-to-use screens, rather than having to know a database language.

In this book we have been using SQL for the examples for the simple reason that it is the most popular database language out there. See chapter 5 for an introduction to SQL. If you are not familiar with SQL, it may be helpful to reference back and forth between this chapter and chapter 5.

SQL is officially defined by the American National Standards Institute (ANSI) and the International Standards Organization (ISO). In practice, I don't think there is any product on the market that follows the latest standard 100%. Different products use different "dialects" that are not compatible with each other. For our purposes here, I will limit the examples to features that should work in almost any SQL product.

15.5. Implement Data Types

The first step is to translate the data types of the columns into SQL data types.

Text columns become "char" or "varchar". Numeric columns become "integer" or "numeric" or "decimal". Dates and times become "date" or "time" or "timestamp".

You may have data types that are not directly implemented in SQL. Many things that users think of as a data type are really just units of measure. For example, a data type of "temperature" is just a number that we understand as "degrees Fahrenheit" or "degrees Celsius". These are easily expressed with one of the number data types. Other "data types" are descriptions of the sort of value that is meaningful. For example, as far as the database is concerned, "telephone number" is a character string with a certain format. Our programs may enforce this format or they may accept any character string and leave it to a human user to decide if it makes sense. In these cases, we select a SQL data type that can hold the sort of values that we need.

Some missing data types really do have storage or processing implications. Still, it is often possible to "simulate" missing data types with existing ones.

For example, many database products do not have any "boolean" or "logical" datatype. This is not a big problem. It is easy enough to define a column as "char(1)" and use some standard values for true and false, like "Y" and "N" or "T" and "F"; or to use an integer with 1 for true and 0 for false.

Other missing data types can be more of a problem. I don't think any database product I've used as an explicit "image" data type. Many have a "binary large object block", or "BLOB", that can hold image data. But I've never actually done it that way. What I've always done is use a varchar to hold the path to a data file that contains the image. (Note: I'm not saying that using a blob to hold image data is a bad idea, just that's it's never proven useful in the applications I've done.)

Some missing data types are only a problem in that we need to nail down exactly what our requirements are. Consider "color". If we are building an order entry system and we need a Color column where users can specify what color skirt or hat they want to buy, than this is simply a varchar column that contains values like "green" or "burgundy" or whatever fancy names for colors we are using this year. If this is a system to control a color printer or paint mixing machine, we need some sort of numerical representation, such as the relative proportion of each of the primary colors.

15.6. Implement Tables

We should already know all the tables and all the columns from our physical model. Once we know the data types, implementing the tables is a matter of writing a SQL "create" statement. This should be a direct translation process with no creativity involved.

At this point the only decision left to be made should be exact table and column names. These must, of course, conform to the naming rules of our database product. SQL normally allows names to include letters, digits, and underscores but no other special characters. SQL is not normally case-sensitive, and many SQL products will translate all names internally to all upper case or all lower case. The C/Java style naming convention of using "camel case" -- capital letters within names as a visual break, like "CustomerBalanceDue" (or "camelCase") -- doesn't work in SQL. It ends up "CUSTOMERBALANCEDUE" which can be difficult to read. We must either simply accept the run-on names, or break the words up with underscores.

For example, suppose our Entity-Attribute List looks like this:

```
Customer (customer number*, first name, last
name, address, city, state, zip code, balance
due)
```

We have determined that the data types are:

customer number	sequential integer
first name	alpha, max 20
last name	alpha, max 40
address	alpha, max 40
city	alpha, max 30
state	alpha, exactly 2
zip code	alpha, exactly 5
balance due	decimal, 5 before and 2 after decimal point

Then our create statement would look like this:

```
create table customer
(customer_number integer,
first_name varchar(20),
last_name varchar(40),
address varchar(40),
city varchar(30),
state char(2),
zip char(5),
balance decimal(7,2))
```

15.7. Implement Primary Keys

Next we want to add the primary key.

```
alter table customer add primary key
(customer_number)
```

Recall that when there is more than one column, we simply separate them with commas. For example, if we had an Order Line table with a key of Order Number plus Line Number, our SQL might be:

```
alter table order_line add primary key
(order_number, line_number)
```

15.8. Implement Foreign Keys

Recall that (most) SQL engines provide some support for managing foreign keys. At this point, we must decide if we want to take advantage of this or manage them ourselves.

As mentioned in chapter 5, the advantage of managing foreign keys in code is that it gives us complete control, and allows us to handle difficult cases in any way that we want. The advantage of letting SQL manage foreign keys is that we declare the relationships in one place rather than every place in the code that manipulates key values, so the opportunity for errors is much less.

If we decide to have SQL manage our foreign keys, we must next decide which update and declare options to select. This depends on the context. The first thing to look at is the obligation of the relationship.

If it is obligatory on the side with the foreign key, then we probably want to use "cascade" on both deletes and updates. If it is illegal to have, say, a Customer Order record with no matching Customer record, then if the Customer is deleted, it makes sense to automatically delete all of his orders. If a Customer is renumbered, we want to keep his orders connected to him.

If the relationship is non-obligatory, we're more likely to want to "on delete set null" so that we don't lose data.

Beyond that you really need to examine what you are doing on a case-by-case basis.

So in our Customer / Customer Order example, we would probably want to say:

```
alter table customer_order
add foreign key (customer_number) references
customer (customer_number) on delete cascade on
update cascade
```

But bear in mind that cascades can update or delete a lot of data. Even if a strict interpretation of the obligation of the relationships says that all child records should be deleted when the parent is deleted, we might want to consider the question: What if the user accidentally deletes a record? Do we want to wipe out hundreds or thousands of records with one keystroke? This becomes more of a programming question than a database design question, but the common answer is to warn the user about dangerous deletes, like displaying a message that says "If you delete this Department record, 3247 Customer records will also be deleted. Do you want to proceed?"

15.9. Create Indexes

In a SQL database, indexes are purely a performance issue. There is no query or other function that will not work because an index is or is not present. The only difference is how fast it runs and how much disk space it takes.

In this book we are discussing how to design a database and not the code that will access that database. Still, by the time you reach this point, you probably have a good idea what queries you will be writing. Many will be obvious. We will almost surely routinely access the Customer table by account number and by the customer's last name. It is unlikely that we will ever access Customers by middle initial or check number used on last payment. Other access paths may not be so obvious and will have to wait until we have written some programs. Will we access Customers by date of first order? That doesn't sound likely, but what if we routinely make special offers to our oldest customers to reward and encourage loyalty?

Fortunately in SQL we can create the tables and obvious indexes now and defer creating additional indexes until we are in to the programming stage. We can also easily drop indexes that we discover we don't need.

So at this point: Create the obvious indexes, but don't worry about it very much.

15.10. Create Sequences

As we discussed in chapter 9, synthetic keys are often sequence numbers: 1, 2, 3, etc. We need a way to assign sequence numbers to new records with no possibility that the same sequence number will be assigned to two different records, even if multiple users or processes are creating new records at the same time.

There are two ways to do this.

The easier way is to use the SQL "sequence" feature. See section 5.7. We then let SQL manage the sequence. We just ask for the next number when we need it.

The other way is to manage the sequence numbers ourselves. Create a table to hold the next available sequence number. Then whenever a new sequence number is needed, retrieve the next available sequence number from this table and then add one to the value so the next try gets a different number. Make sure you understand the "locking" mechanism of your database so that two processes cannot be assigned the same number.

It is common to create a single table for all sequence numbers. This table has two columns: one for a name or identifier of the sequence, and the other to hold the next available number. (You can either store the last number you assigned, or the next number available to be assigned. It doesn't much matter, just be sure you always use it the same way.)

If our sequence numbers are complex, we may be forced to manage them ourselves. Some dialects of SQL allow for more complex rules about sequence numbers, but if it goes past a simple count for each table, we probably want to just do it ourselves.

The most common complexity is the need to assign sequence numbers within a series or grouping. For example, perhaps we want the customer identifier to be office number, hyphen, sequence. In that case we need to maintain a separate sequence for each office. That requires a table that holds office number and next sequence number. If we already have an Office table, we may put it in there, or we may create a new table for this.

Sometimes we get blocks of sequence numbers from some outside organization. For example, devices on the Internet – computers, routers, printers, etc -- are each assigned an Internet Protocol (IP) address. Each owner of a network can request a series of numbers that they can assign to their devices from one of the international standards organizations that manages these. (For example in North America, it's ARIN, the American Registry for Internet Numbers.) If you run out, you can go back and request another block. So a database to assign and manage IP addresses for your network would have to start with the first block, work its way through until that block is all used up, and then start on the next block. SQL sequences are not going to handle this. You would have to create tables and write code to manage it yourself.

15.11. Review Questions

1. What does it mean to get "prematurely physical"?

2. What can we do when our database engine does not support a data type we used in our model? (Consider Booleans and images as examples.)

3. What is a "foreign key"?

4. When might we want to use a sequence? When do we need to manage sequence numbers ourselves?

16. FLEXING THE MODEL

The Sabbath was made for man, and not man for the Sabbath.

-- Mark 2:27 (NKJV)

16.1. Introduction

We have discussed a lot of rules for designing databases. But the purpose of these rules is to help us do our jobs. The purpose of our jobs is not to uphold the rules.

What happens when following the rules makes your job harder? The answer is simple: Break the rules.

Many database designers refer to breaking the rules as "denormalization". This term is misleading because it implies that the rules we are breaking are the rules of normalization, when in fact there are any number of others rules equally worthy of being broken. I prefer the term "flexing the model". I haven't seen this term used frequently, but I think it's more descriptive.

Of course you should be very slow to break the rules. They represent years of experience by many smart people. They're usually – almost always – good ideas. But "almost always" is not "always".

Especially if you're new at this, start out trying to follow the rules. Don't break the rules until it's very, very clear that they are causing you trouble. As you gain experience, you'll get a better feel for when the rules should be broken.

When in doubt, follow the rules.

All those cautions taken, when should you break the rules?

16.2. Redundant Data and Performance

Perhaps the most common reason to break the rules is because of performance issues. And perhaps the most common rule to break for performance reasons is the rule against redundant data. Sometimes data that is technically redundant is nevertheless so difficult or time-consumiing to calculate that, for practical purposes, we give up and store it twice.

Suppose you are designing a system for a bank. The system must keep a complete history of all the deposits, withdrawals, and any other transactions that have ever been made against a customer's account. We will occasionally ask for details of a five-year-old transaction, so we have to keep it. But among the most common questions your staff and customers ask is, "What is this customer's current balance?" If we have all the transactions, then keeping the current balance is redundant: We could always calculate it by adding up all the deposits and subtracting all the withdrawals and adding or subtracting any other adjustments made since the customer opened the account. But if the customer has had an account for years, this could be hundreds or thousands of transactions. If it is a business customer, they could have hundreds of transactions a day. Doing all this totaling every time we need to calculate a balance would likely be a serious performance drag. If any record in that entire history is ever lost or damaged, the total will be wrong.

An obvious solution is to violate the rule against redundant data and store the current balance separately, and update it as each transaction is added to the system.

Adventures
in Real Life!

In a medical office management system, we routinely produced statements showing a patient's previous balance, new charges and payments since the last statement, and new balance.

Rather than recalculate the balance from scratch every time, we stored the balance from each statement on the database. For a statement we would then start from the last balance record and finish up by making a new one. To determine a customer's current balance, we found the most recent balance and then added in any transactions after that date.

We did make one bad decision: We stored the balance records in the transaction table along with charges and payments. So any attempt to add up amounts had to have a check for balance records so it could exclude them, or transactions would effectively be counted twice. We should have created a separate "balance table".

This breaks all the rules against redundancy, but it is extremely practical when accounts have a lot of activity.

16.3. Unnormalized Data and Performance

Similarly, sometimes technically correct normalization leads to performance problems.

Adventures
in Real Life!

I worked on a system for a chain of retail stores. The stores kept records about what merchandise they had in stock. Each store had various "locations" – display area, rooms and shelves in the back, sometimes warehouse space. Stores were then grouped into regions.

We had a Stock table that recorded the current location of each product in stock. By normalization rules, if we wanted

---

to know the store, we could find it by looking up the location. If we wanted to know the region, we could find it by looking up the store.

But regions routinely shared their stock, so when they checked for "on hand" items they wanted to know if it was at any store in the region. Most functions involving stock looked at an entire region. In a fully normalized database, this means we would be constantly doing four-table joins on Stock, Location, Store, and Region. That would be very slow. The more practical solution was to accept a slight amount of unnormalization and store an extra copy of the region code in the stock record.

16.4. Concatenated Keys and Convenience

In section 8.3 I warned against cramming multiple facts into a single attribute. As I noted, there are many reasons not to do this. But there is one time when it can be a good idea: When the attribute is the table's primary key.

When a primary key contains multiple columns, every time we need to join that table to another we have to match on all these columns. This can be a pain. If we cram all the columns into one, then we only have one column to match on and life is simpler.

Example: We have an Order table whose primary key is Customer plus Order Date plus Sequence Number. Every time we want to link another table to Order, we have to manipulate three columns. In our queries we are repeatedly writing things like "where lineitem.customer = order.customer and lineitem.orderdate = order.orderdate and lineitem.sequence = customer.sequence". It's tedious and creates the possibility that we will forget one. So instead, we create a concatenated column that crams these three things together, probably with some separator character between them, so we get keys like "JS983234/2008-04-12/001".

An obvious alternative to this technique is to create a synthetic key to use as the primary key instead. If you find yourself creating three separate columns because you need to manipulate the columns individually, and then also cramming them together into a

---

concatenated column for the key, it may be easier to just make the primary key a simple sequence number.

16.5.   System Tables

In chapter 5, Entities, I said that an entity must have identifiable occurrences. That is, there must be more than one of them.

But sometimes we have general "system data" that we need to store somewhere. Things like our own company's address or our account number with the credit card clearing house. We only have one copy of the system and one "our company", so by the rules we can't create a "system" or "our company" entity, because there is only one instance. But we need to store this data somewhere. We don't want to hard-code it in the program: it's certainly possible that we'll move the main office some day or switch to another credit card clearing house.

(It is not an answer to say that there may be other organizations that also own a copy of this software product, and therefore there are multiple instances of "company". Our copy of the database is our universe. We don't care what is happening in other universes. If something that they're doing is of interest to us, than it had better be in our database.)

So sometimes it's a good idea to break the rule about identifiable occurrences, and allow a "system" table with just one record.

16.6.   What Not

Other special cases may arise from time to time. If we could list them all, we could make rules for them, and they wouldn't be special cases. Use your judgment, and evaluate them on a case-by-case basis.

16.7.   Review Questions

1.   Why is it okay to break the rules sometimes?

2.   When is redundant data good?

3.   When are concatenated columns good?

Index

www.ingramcontent.com/pod-product-compliance
Lightning Source LLC
Chambersburg PA
CBHW051237050326
40689CB00007B/963